A Directors Guild of America Publication

WENDELL FRANKLIN

Interviewed by Zeinabu Davis

1995 Directors Guild of America, Inc.

First edition 1995.

Library of Congress Catalog Card Number: 94-074712.

ISBN 1-882766-01-6

1. Wendell Franklin, 1916–1994—Interview. 2. Motion picture directors—United States. 3. Black studies—History. 4. Los Angeles—History. 5. Black filmmakers—History.

A Directors Guild of America Publication
7920 Sunset Boulevard
Los Angeles, California 90046

Wendell Franklin, 1985.

For Adam-Brant Franklin Smith

— *Wendell Franklin*

TABLE OF CONTENTS

continued

ACKNOWLEDGMENTS

Wendell Franklin was interviewed by Zeinabu Davis in 1987 as part of the Directors Guild of America Oral History Series, which chronicles the lives and careers of pioneer DGA members in the fields of motion pictures, television, and radio. This ongoing program is under the auspices of Directors Guild of America, Special Projects, headed by National Special Projects Officer Selise E. Eiseman.

When Wendell Franklin joined the DGA in 1960, he made history, becoming the Guild's first African-American member, and he made history again — and gained national media coverage — when he was chosen as an assistant director by director George Stevens on *The Greatest Story Ever Told*.

Sadly, Mr. Franklin died in July of 1994, before this book was printed, although he was able to read the edited manuscript, and looked forward to its publication. After his death, several friends and colleagues assisted in the completion of this volume: DGA member William Crain; Horace Jackson; Stanley G. Robertson; and especially, Lily Smith, who graciously gathered and allowed us access to many original photographs.

Others who were integral to the project and otherwise helped in the manuscript's preparation include: David Shepard who originally commissioned the interview for the DGA; Kevin Hindley, who shaped the book into its present chapter format; editorial assistant and researcher Irina Ozernoy; and editorial assistant Nancy E. Walsh.

— *Adele Field, DGA Oral Histories Editor*

PREFACE

by STANLEY G. ROBERTSON

When I received the call from a longtime friend, Eunice Lubin, on that hot July Friday afternoon in the summer of 1994, that Wendell Franklin had "just passed away," it was an emotional body blow from which I have not as yet recovered. I had known that Wendell was ill, hospitalized for several weeks, but his death was totally unexpected as far as I was concerned. I had spoken to him just a day or two earlier; even though it was difficult for him to speak, and that once booming, joy-filled voice was only a whisper of what it had been, Wendell was full of the humor and optimism which were mainstays of his life. But, Wendell gone? At the time, it was difficult to accept. It still is, even though I realize I should have long passed through the "period of denial" which psychiatrists explain is one of the early stages we humans pass through in coming to the realization that a loved one is no longer with us. As we are taught in our earliest and most fundamental teachings, each living thing which inhabits the earth must one day die; but some people seem indestructible, gifted with the mantle of perennial Springtime, never imagined in the Winter of their years with life's juices slowly fading to black.

Such a person was Wendell James Franklin.

For those oh so few African Americans who began to crack the odious racial barriers of the motion picture and television industry in the 1950s, he was Our Beacon, Our True Role Model in the classical sense of the expression. For those of us who grew up in the minuscule African American community of Los Angeles before and during the Second World War — there were "39,000 Negroes" estimated to be in the city according to the 1940 census — Wendell Franklin preached the gospel of the optimist; that there was "a new day coming," and to be ready for it you had to prepare yourself by more than dreaming and wishing.

To say that Wendell Franklin was not colorful, controversial, charismatic, moody, no saint, a man who sometimes talked when he should have listened, impulsive and security conscious at the same time, or as complex a man as one would ever hope to meet, yet one with simplistic values, motives and dreams, is like saying beach front property in Malibu is cheap. You didn't know Wendell and you obviously don't know your real estate if you are in agreement with the above statement.

I'd heard about Wendell long before I ever met him. It was difficult not to be aware of him and his exploits if you were a young Black man growing up with dreams of wanting to do something in the entertainment business in the Los Angeles area following the Second World War. I was first introduced to Wendell by the late Jessie Mae Brown-Beavers, the legendary and famed Society Editor of the now defunct *California Eagle* newspaper, and later the Woman's Page Editor of *The Los Angeles Sentinel* newspaper. Mrs. Brown-Beavers, who aided so many in launching their careers (including me), was one of those people who was so well-known in the community that one had only to identify her by her first name — "Jessie

Mae" — and she was immediately recognizable. For almost five decades — beginning when she was a student at UCLA — she was truly the social arbiter of Black Los Angeles and an important leader in political, cultural and philanthropic circles in the greater Los Angeles community which reached far beyond the restrictive ethnic confines of the period.

I was attending school and trying to fashion a career in journalism which I hoped would one day lead to an opportunity in the motion picture and television industry to which I had been exposed as a child through my mother's working for a number of film celebrities, including Joan Crawford, Franchot Tone, the Riskin family of writer Robert and producer Everett, and several others. Unlike many Black "celebrities" of the period — and Wendell was truly a "celebrity" in our community — Wendell was very encouraging and supportive of my dreams and ambitions when Jessie Mae introduced us and told him of my aspirations. Until his dying day, through some good times and bad, Wendell was always that way. Also, when we first met, he displayed something to me which was a characteristic so typical of him: he treated me, a kid with barely one good suit, as if I were as important to him as the richest and most influential mogul in Hollywood. Beginning in a period long before "Black is Beautiful" and "I am somebody" were fashionable, Wendell, by his actions or attitudes, infused all he touched or came in contact with, with this philosophy. He would have it no other way, and would not allow anyone in his presence to think or act otherwise, whether talking to a group of interracial and unenlightened college students, the most hardlined bigots who make up some of the crews of the most successful television series and films, the ultra-conservative and reactionary members of some of the top unions and guilds in the entertainment industry, or "preaching to the choir" of those who agreed with him and what he stood for.

To those without a knowledge of history, or who are so self-involved that their egos will not allow them to look beyond the latest story about themselves in the "trade papers," it may seem that to appreciate what Wendell Franklin accomplished, or what greater triumphs might have been his had the proverbial "playing field" been level, one has to examine with an objective eye the period in which Wendell James Franklin grew up and came to maturity in. For some, they were the "good old days." But those "some" were not African Americans, and did not dream of and strive towards establishing a "creative career" in the motion picture and television industry. People in the Entertainment Industry speak of the "Glory Days" of motion pictures — the Twenties, Thirties and Forties. They also speak of "Television's Golden Age," the 1950s. However, they were not "Golden" or "Glory" years for people of color. In his book, *Moving Pictures,* the famous and award-winning writer Budd Schulberg, whose father, B. P. Schulberg, was the Production Head of Paramount Pictures during a major portion of the 1920s and '30s, says that the "only" Black person he remembers seeing working on the Paramount lot was a guy who shined shoes at the gate and was the butt of practical jokes. At MGM, the fair lair of the most successful mogul of moguls, Louis B. Mayer, who boasted that "there are more stars at MGM than in God's Heaven," again, except for the guy who shined shoes, there were no African Americans regularly employed during the studio's heyday. When the Second World War came along and it became difficult to get workers, the studios made a "concession" and began hiring Blacks as janitors and to do maintenance work.

Today, much is made of the "high points" television achieved during the 1950s through its landmark dramas, cultural affairs programming, and the introduction of such programming concepts as *Today*, *Wide, Wide World*, *Omnibus*, and the nightly news programs on a nationwide basis. Yet, for instance, it was not until the late 1950s that NBC in Los Angeles began hiring Blacks for anything more than parking lot attendants, mailroom clerks, pages in their guest relations department, and stenographic department clerks. And it was the most progressive of the network flagship operations in Hollywood, thanks primarily to a strong willed and fair minded NBC West Coast Executive Vice President named John K. West, and the work of the then local Executive Director of the Los Angeles Urban League, the late and celebrated Wesley Brazier. I remember vividly being told by the head of ABC's Employment Department, in the summer of 1957 when I was fresh out of the University of Southern California's Telecommunications Department and looking for a job, that "I can't hire you because if I did, I would have to hire another Negro so you'd have somebody to talk to!" At CBS, during the same period, I remember filling out an application for employment and watching a woman, who was a middle level employee, after interviewing me, toss my application in the waste basket in front of me. She did the same thing on several different occasions, and when I complained to her boss, he replied, "So what?"

I know that some of those younger Blacks, who met Wendell when he was in retirement and several years past a day-to-day involvement in the art of filmmaking, thought that he was "passé," "a little past it," or worse, "old-fashioned." Wrong: nothing could be further from the truth. I remember talking to a young Black woman last year who is involved in the entertainment industry and who had heard Wendell speak at a meeting of Black film professionals. "Too bad he wasn't more militant when it mattered. If he had used some of the tactics we're using today, things might have been different for him," she said before I cut her off and gave her a very acidic look at the facts and where she and others like her would be had there been no man like Wendell Franklin.

At a time when no Black person could sit down to eat at the fabled Hollywood dining establishments such as the Brown Derby, Romanoff's, or Chasen's, let alone even one of the studio commissaries, Wendell was working on the Parking Lot at NBC's old Sunset and Vine Radio City, studying his craft through hook or crook means, and raising thousands and thousands of dollars — maybe even hundreds of thousands of dollars — for local Black charitable and civic organizations by putting on stage shows at clubs such as the Florentine Gardens, which allowed people to rent the place when they were "dark!" At a time when there were still residential racial restrictions as to where one could live in Los Angeles — yes, Los Angeles, not Jackson, Miss. — and the daily newspapers advertised "White Only" in their "Help Wanted" columns, Franklin, who had come back from the Second World War with an even deeper desire to crack the entertainment industry than he had had when he marched away, observed staging and camera techniques and all the other things that go into knowing how to put shows and films together with the few established White directors, stage managers, and creative people who would allow him to. He also lobbied, not only for himself, with the executives of NBC to hire and promote more Blacks who were coming out of good schools and who sought a professional opportunity in the business.

I remember that day in August, 1957, when I started at NBC as a page in Guest Relations — only the third Black page hired in the history of NBC — being greeted by Wendell, who had spread the word among the executives at NBC that I was a "young man to keep an eye on." What I told the young woman I spoke to last year was, among other things, that when Wendell, because of his determination and hard work, was promoted from a parking lot supervisor to stage manager, he was only the second Black man in the history of American television to reach this position. Fred Lights, who worked for Dave Garroway and the *Today Show* at NBC in New York, was the first. Wendell was forty-two years old at the time! In 1960, when he became the first African American admitted to the Directors Guild of America, Wendell was forty-four years old, a man who had waited almost two decades for the opportunity.

As I told the young woman I spoke to, I wonder how many of her peers could achieve the success Wendell did under the conditions he was forced — and I do mean forced — to work under once he became a stage manager and assistant director. I never "walked in Wendell's shoes," but I knew much of what he went through, because we remained in touch with one another — professionally and personally — throughout the years. He shared with me many of his innermost thoughts. I wrote several articles on him for *The Los Angeles Sentinel* and other publications. When I produced a series for Universal Television and NBC, he worked as an assistant director on the series. We spent many hours — mostly on the telephone in recent years, as his schedule slowed and mine increased — speaking about what he considered his triumphs and what he felt he still would like to accomplish. I knew the man well. I remember his experience with the late Jack Bailey, the host for the successful daytime show *Queen for a Day,* a show which I remember working on as a page. When Wendell was promoted to stage manager, one of the shows he was assigned to was *Queen for a Day*. (Some of the network-originated shows from NBC West Coast would not take Wendell.) In order to "cue" the models during one segment of the program, the stage manager had to lightly tap the young woman on the shoulder when it was time for her to make her appearance on stage. Seeing Wendell do this — which was verified by others on the show — Bailey, who tried to give the impression to America of what a "swell guy he was," immediately went into a rage and told Wendell loudly and angrily, "Boy, I never want to see you touch a White woman again. If you do, you're fired." Wendell found a way around Bailey's prejudice, as did the models who told Wendell to just "lightly tap on the stage floor; we'll hear you."

I remember the treatment — calling it shabby would be polite — Wendell received from some members of the

Directors Guild who, in a public stance, purported to be in the "forefront of civil rights," but who would not speak to Franklin or employ him on their projects. At a low point, when he had to return to NBC as a Parking Lot Supervisor because he could not get a job in the business, I remember Wendell telling me, "It hurts. It really hurts to talk to people and have them tell you that they're going to hire you and see in their eyes that they're lying, lying just to get you out of their face. It hurts to work together on a project, and then when it's over to see all the White boys working together on the next film and you left out. Or, bumping into somebody you'd worked with on the street or on a lot someplace, and having them completely ignore you or pretend as if they don't know where they know you from. Strange when you spent a lot of time together — weeks and weeks — and you were the only Black person on the film. People ask me why I'm always so happy and with a smile on my face. Well, it's to keep from crying."

As the man said, "It just hurts too bad, but I can't let them see me crying."

But I also remember the joy of the man. I recall and recollect those moments and hours when Wendell, throughout the years, spoke of those whom he would be eternally grateful to, those who had touched his life and made it better, more fruitful, more enjoyable. I remember his pride when he called me and told me he was going to work for the legendary George Stevens on *The Greatest Story Ever Told*. I also remember his joy when, after the film was completed and he invited my wife and I to its premiere, he said, "If I die tomorrow, I have experienced what it's like to work with a true genius, and a man possessed with the utmost professionalism and decency."

As the years went by, Franklin often referred to Stevens as his "creative father."

When John K. West died long after he'd left NBC, Franklin called and said, "I heard that Mr. West (to those of us who were influenced by him, it was always 'Mr. West' out of genuine respect) just passed on. This would be the most beautiful of worlds if just five percent of the people were like he was."

He spoke fondly of Haskell Wexler, with whom he worked on one of the most important films of the last three decades, *Medium Cool*.

"The man is a genius," he said one night shortly after his return to Chicago, where the movie was filmed while it was still in post-production. "I've never learned as much and been treated in such a true collegiate and professional manner as I have been while working with Haskell."

Franklin, who sometimes engaged in exaggeration and momentary enthusiasm, was sincere in his thoughts about Haskell Wexler and *Medium Cool*. He repeated the words many times throughout the years. In early February of 1994, just before he became ill and went into the hospital, we had a long talk about film and movies, as we often did. I told Wendell that I had recently screened *Medium Cool* as a reference point for something I was currently working on. I relayed to him how great it was to see his "credit," and to see, in the eyes of a couple of young executives who were watching the film with me and who had never seen it before, their sincere appreciation for the skillfully done work.

"The man is a true genius," he smiled, repeating the rest of his comments about the fashion in which he was treated and how much he learned.

Wendell had a prodigious memory. He could remember things which happened sixty years ago as if they were yesterday. Even though he had faced much adversity and had had many of his dreams dashed during his lifetime, Wendell had a propensity to only recall vividly the "good," not concentrating on the "bad."

Even though he had said this many times throughout the years — because I had known the man also during our NBC days — Wendell always had great memories of Bill Finnegan, who was a senior stage manager when Wendell broke into the department, and who went out of his way to help him, giving him pointers and guidance while others went out of their way to try to block his progress, hoping that he'd fail. Just before his last illness, Wendell said to me, "I'm happy that Bill Finnegan (now a producer of feature films) is doing so well. He stuck his neck out to help me when those other guys stood in the way. I guess some people do get their just desserts."

I've worked during my career with some of the great filmmakers and directors in the History of the Motion Picture Art. I say this not as a point of braggadocio, but as one of reference. Could Wendell Franklin have been a top film director? Absolutely! Had it not been for the accident of parentage, and the vagaries of the time, Wendell could have done it! There's no question in my mind based on my experience of having seen the works of an overwhelming majority of American and foreign filmmakers of note since the art form became a reality. He had the flair, the style, the visual eye, and the knowledge and understanding of the human condition and its foibles and eccentricities. He had the energy and curiosity, the love of the filmmaking process, the temperamental mood swings and ego, the charismatic influence on other people, and the dedication to completing something under the most difficult conditions that all top filmmakers and directors possess and have had to possess.

Also, he had the other ingredient that everyone who ever thought that he could entertain others has had: the ability to bounce back after failure. To never doubt one's own ability and vision, regardless of what others might say or think.

Hollywood is an image and perception town. Many have the "image" of being successful when they're not. If the "perception" of you is one held in high esteem by those who are the "current power brokers," then you must be highly regarded. And, with these "images" and "perceptions" come the accouterments of both: the "right table" at the "right restaurant" at the "right time." The "corner office" in the "right building." The name on the "A" invitation list. Your film occupying "the billboard" on Sunset Boulevard when it's released. Wendell achieved the latter honor when *The Bus Is Coming*, produced by Horace Jackson and directed by Wendell Franklin, became the subject matter of "the billboard."

This was the early 1970s, and Wendell called and asked if I'd seen it. I told him I had not. He wanted to "rent a limousine" and take me by. "Baby," he said joyfully, "It'll be great driving by that billboard, drinking champagne and thinking of where we've come from." I declined the offer, but my wife and I made a special trip from our then home in the West San Fernando Valley to see it. It was a true delight for me, because if anyone deserved it, Wendell did.

I called him to express my pleasure and he replied, "Don't you think that next time, my name should be more distinctive, stand out a little more?"

I had to laugh; that was Wendell. Unfortunately, there was no "next time." Wendell never directed another picture, although he continued to work for years as an assistant director.

However, in the history of Hollywood, his name will always be distinctive, and stand out!

PROLOGUE

It seems like just a few afternoons ago that I was ensconced in one of Sunset Strip's very plush clubs at an invitational luncheon hosted by Robert Wise, the past President of the Directors Guild of America (DGA) and current President of the Academy of Motion Picture Arts and Sciences. Here was a room of many distinguished people honoring a fine gentleman, David Shepard, who was leaving the position of Special Projects Officer at the DGA.

In the room were George Sidney, the director of *Bye, Bye, Birdie*; Arthur Hiller of *Love Story*; distinguished members from the university campuses of UCLA and USC; and other prominent inside people of the industry called motion pictures. Here were many people the world would like to touch hands with, and yet I felt that I was alone in this room. After much conversation here and there I found myself socially isolated in a strange way. Oh, there were greetings and handshakes, but all of a sudden the conversation died and they would go on to other colleagues who were very much involved with them and their various enterprises and projects.

In a room of over 150 people there was only one other black man — the director, William Crain — a black associate director, Gina Gates — and two very lovely black ladies who were staff of the Directors Guild of America.

I looked around and said, "Are we the only five who are on an invitational list within the closed circles of 'Hollywood,' if you will?" After the event, I meandered down Sunset Strip and I began to look backwards in my life; over 45 years within the entertainment industry with over 30 years behind the camera. I pondered this thought: *I'm still alone as I was in the beginning. I'm still an isolated person. Why?* I can't explain it, except for my color. Blacks are accepted to a point, but we're not a part of the mainstream establishment; not an equal part of the motion picture industry.

This is the essence of my story: a black man within the industry.

CHILDHOOD

I first saw the light of day in Los Angeles, California, in the year 1916, the date, November 15. I was the proud baby boy of John and Birdie Hightower, and my given name was Gordon. My birth mother and father were in show business at the time. Birdie was with the leading travelling black shows of the time, *Stepping High* and *Shuffle Along*.

At that time show business was big among blacks; there were nightclubs all across the country in the various cities where there was room for black entertainers. Back then you had a more cohesive black community in America. During the teens, there were the famed Silas Green Minstrel shows and they used to have what they called "chautaquas." They used to set up a big tent and put on minstrel shows. This was a really big event.

The whites would do the same thing in the Ziegfeld Theater, with Eddie Cantor and Al Jolson performing in black face. That was something else that the Anglo had taken from the blacks; it originated in the minstrel shows. There was very little around as far as theaters go. Movies were just beginning in the teens and early twenties. So the stage was the biggest form of visual entertainment that involved blacks.

I'm sure that like many young people today, my birth parents were enamored of show business and along came little Gordon — a baby who was going to be a burden on them.

The people who were destined to become my parents were leading hotel, restaurant and nightclub owners in Los Angeles. John and Birdie Hightower were staying at their hotel and Mrs. Franklin had become attached to their baby. Thus, Mr. and Mrs. Henry James (Jim) Franklin applied for the adoption of Gordon Hightower. They became my legal parents when I was two years and eight months old, on July 13, 1919. My name was officially changed to Wendell Gordon Franklin.

I did not know I was adopted until I was 21 years old. Since then, I cared less about pursuing it, because I think when you're adopted, your birth parents lose their rights. She's not my mother, she just gave birth to me. I mean that's the way I've accepted it. The Franklins are the ones who paid for me all my life, the doctor bills, the food and clothes, and college. They were my parents.

They had bought property in 1889, on West 22nd Street close to Vermont, in an all-white neighborhood. I don't know how they managed to get the property and build, because it was a great shock to the neighbors when they found out that a black family had built this beautiful home. They thought that my mother, Mrs. Franklin, was the maid. My father, Jim Franklin, was a very serious man. Now I knew there was a little of the player in him; he was too handsome and too pretty. My mother had a fancy for tall, good looking men, and he had the right color and the "good" hair. My mother once said this to me about my real mother and father: "You got white folks on the back of your head, but you got a little nigger on each side." Apparently, Mr. Franklin was a very distinguished looking man of Indian, Spanish and Creole background; he looked anything other than what a black man should look like; at least according to white people's definitions. Remember we didn't use the word black in the twenties; your behind would get kicked fifty thousand times, if you called somebody black, it was really an insult.

Birdie, my birth mother, was hired as a nurse for me. She stayed with the Franklins as my nurse up until 1921. In the meantime, she and John Hightower were divorced, and Birdie married again. She married a top Broadway entertainer and dancer by the name of Duke Williams. Through that union there was a male child who is my half brother. His name was also Duke Williams. They moved out to a place over the Rosebud Theater, on Central Avenue and Twentieth Street, which was practically an all-white neighborhood at that time. These were considered very smart apartments at that time.

Birdie Hightower died at a very young age. My brother was adopted by my father's sister and they moved to San Francisco. I've lost track of whatever happened to him. I've had several letters in recent years, of men who claim to be my brother, especially after I received national publicity, but I have never been able to ascertain it legally. Relatives come out of the woodwork when they think that you're getting ahead.

My parents came to Los Angeles from St. Louis, and Little Rock, Arkansas. I have a great aunt who taught at the University of Arkansas, the same place where black kids were turned away by Governor Wallace. Everybody migrated out of the deep south, to New York and Chicago. Others became servants to people in Washington. I think General Washington would drop dead now to see all those black men sitting up in Congress in Washington. The Constitution wasn't written for my folks — we were still in slavery. It was written for the other folks.

Apparently, the Franklins had good businesses in St. Louis and they also operated a saloon back in 1901 and 1902 in Las Vegas, right where the Fremont Hotel is now. I went up there in the middle years of my life and met the old sheriff who knew my father. He said we never should have sold the property there. Every time my mother made a little money, she'd go and invest in property there. People of that time were very conscious of land. That was the dream of all citizens — to own a piece of the soil.

The Bronx Hotel, which was on Seventh Street, was controlled and owned by my parents. The Franklins were an affluent family, and many show business people stopped at the hotel. One of the most enterprising professions among blacks, especially black men, was to be a Pullman car porter or a dining car waiter, and they made fabulous money. Airplanes hadn't come in vogue yet. Right down Fifth Street to Central Avenue was the Union Station, where trains came into Los Angeles. The Bronx Hotel was the haven for all the people who were on the railroad or in show business. This was before the Somerville was built, which was to eventually become the Dunbar Hotel on Central Avenue, another black show business haven.

The Bronx Hotel had about a hundred rooms, which was quite large at that time. My mother and father ran it together, along with the nightclub in the hotel, the Palms Garden. They also ran two restaurants in other parts of the city, the Little Jim Cafes, named after my father. One was on Twelfth and Central, the other on Twentieth and

Central. I only came down to the hotel maybe on the weekend, on a Saturday afternoon and sometimes they would let me stay up and watch the club show. Curtis Mosby's orchestra played in the nightclub and when the Alabam opened next door to the Dunbar Hotel, Curtis took over that club with his orchestra.

Everything was all in the same area in downtown Los Angeles; going from the Union Station to Seventh and Broadway would just take about ten or fifteen minutes. All the big time theaters were on Broadway, Hill and Main Streets. On Main Street there was the Burbank Theater, the Follies, the Hippodrome, the Mason Opera House. On Broadway was the Orpheum, the Majestic, the Palace, the Million Dollar, all vaudeville houses. Over on Hill Street was the RKO, also a vaudeville house. Every so often there would be black artists on these predominantly white shows.

I remember seeing Bert Williams, who was a part of Williams and Walker on the RKO or Keith circuit. Many of the artists were staying at my parents' hotel and as I grew older they would take me with them to the matinees. I would sit backstage in the dressing rooms and see the shows from the wings. One was Josephine Baker's *Shuffle Along*, which my birth mother, Birdie, was working on as a wardrobe mistress. I was instilled in music and opera as a kid. I remember seeing Leopold Stokowski conduct the premiere of William Grant Still's Afro-American Symphony of Tuscany at the Pan-Pacific Auditorium. Seeing him and the whole orchestra perform and the standing ovation they got was a great moment of my youth. So this was the first bit of show biz blood poisoning I received.

In vaudeville, they always had seven or eight acts after the motion picture. When you went to the show then, you had the newsreel, the coming attractions, the serial, a comedy, a cartoon and finally the feature picture. The band played in a pit. Vaudeville was like a talent search show. I mean it was just act after act, with the big star of the show appearing last. After the big act it was time to go home, unless you were going to sit through another show. So the first show would be about ten o'clock and the first afternoon show would be about two o'clock, then they played the picture, then the next show would be at about five thirty. The eight o'clock show was always different, because kids didn't go to the eight o'clock show. Anything risqué would be at the eight o'clock show. After the last vaudeville show you would be into the picture, so you were there for another three hours of films. You got your money's worth when you went to the show then. Many a time they used to come looking for me on the front row at six o'clock in the evening, as I would stay through the second show.

Saturday night would be the real Talent Night. The first time I won something was when they had nine of us kids on the stage at the Boulevard Theater to see who could eat a mouthful of crackers and whistle first. I won the first prize of ten dollars. Later, I was in a big show called "The Kiddies Minstrels," which was produced at the Philharmonic Auditorium by two women by the names of Lauretta Butler and Alma Hightower. They used to get the children from all the families that could afford it and give them dancing and singing lessons. After a certain number of lessons, we would begin to prepare for our show. I'll never forget when I was ten years old, I was in the first part of the show, and I sang with a full orchestra "Honey, I'm in love with you honey, say it isn't funny..."

I had a very encouraging family; so long as I wanted to do things and advance myself, there was nothing they didn't give me within reason. What was affordable, I got. Emma Franklin was a very prudent woman with money and when times were hard, rather than go on welfare, she spread the word to other people who worked in service, so that she would do the shirts of their employers. Nevertheless, I want you to know that laundry was delivered to the back door! Emma was not letting anything through the front door. She wouldn't let it touch her there. Many of these women did sewing and ironing to maintain the fact that they were not going to go on welfare.

I can still see my mother with as many as a hundred shirts. At the time we had a little laundry room, and sometimes the white folks would drive by to pick up the old man's shirts. They drove up in the driveway, and went to the front door. Emma would go to the front door and see them, "Oh, I've come to pick up Mr. So-and-so's..." She said, "Up the driveway, please," and some of those white people got really insulted. She had all the tradesmen come to the back door too. She was that kind of woman.

My mother married again after my father passed away in 1931. There were two sides to the family she married into, the white side and the black side. My stepfather, Howard Smart came from the white side. They were rough tooting cowboys; they used to ride in with their horses down on Main Street, so they went way, way back. Reputedly, their family was the first black family, their first baby was the first black child to be born in Los Angeles and the third in California. They owned the Smart Ranch, which ran from 90th and Figueroa to 100th and Figueroa. Great grandfather Smart had four wives at the same time, with children by each. Polygamy was big at that time.

Most of the black people and families of that time were independent. Families used to exchange pies and cakes, and that's when clothing hung out on the line. I had to do certain chores. For instance, before I went to school on Monday, I had to be up in time to help my mother with the old fashioned Maytag washing machine. We thought we were so straight when we had an electric washing machine and the rollaway. You just put the sheets in and it turned automatically, but I had to put those hems together on the line before I went to school, and when I got home at three o'clock I had to take them off and fold them. When you took them off the line, you had to be careful, so when you brought them in, they would look like they were practically ironed. But all these sheets had to be ironed, there were no rough dried sheets.

Both my mother and father were prominent in the community, my dad being a 33rd degree Mason and a Shriner. My mother was a matron of the Eastern Star, and was a member of the Elks. She was also on the many boards of the church. She was quite involved in women's community clubs and helped set up the Sojourner Truth Home for Girls in the middle of the Depression. I guess I get a lot of arrogance and snobbery from my family because they taught me that I was just as good as anybody else, and not to think otherwise.

One day I got in a fight with a white boy and he chased me home. I ran in the back door screaming "Momma, Momma!" and she said, "What's the matter?" I said, "Howard was chasing me!" "Well you chase him back, 'cause you not getting in this house, till you do." I got news for you, I chased him back up the street. If I didn't whip his ass, I was going to get my ass whipped when I got home. I've always remembered that incident, and consequently I've always felt equal to anybody, be they black, white, green or whatever. Now that's the way I was raised.

There was nothing that I did that my parents weren't there for, from graduations to Children's Day. I can see myself with the teacher, Mrs. Parker, who gave me two little verses to memorize for the recital, and I can hear my father calling on the phone: "Mrs. Paaarker, what is this you just gave my son. Just these two little stanzas? I want something for him to get up there for." Then I'd come home with a poem fifty miles long. Momma rehearsed me and rehearsed me and rehearsed me. She would end up knowing the poem better than I did. But I knew that if I messed up real bad, I was going to get it. My mother used to sit down and say "Wendell, why don't you read tonight for us?" If I made a mistake in pronunciation, she'd correct me. This is where my theatrical nature began to be nurtured. I think that's one reason why I'm a good speaker — I can stop a room and I'm loud.

Momma was a stickler when I came home with my school work; she would sit down with me and make sure I got it done and done right. Now, I don't feel that she had any great college education. At that time in 1925, very few blacks finished anybody's college. They went to normal school, they went to eighth grade. Boys learned trades like woodshop and printing. Girls had to go to sewing, homemaking and cooking classes. That was a requirement in high school. Now we had all of the other electives, glee club, drama, Spanish club, and literature club, but you had to take certain requisites in the public school, and consequently that gave you some intuition that everybody was not going to be bankers and lawyers. Now this was not a matter of black and white, this was a matter of what was taught.

When I was about eight years old, the custom was to have an "acidity" [asafetida—ED.] bag put around your neck in a little tobacco sack. Acidity kept colds and the flu down. It's a herbal concoction and you could smell it for blocks! In a whole classroom of white students, there would be four or five of us blacks wearing asafetida. You had to wear this every year and then you had to have a "cleaning out" — an enema — just before Easter. That's when all the carpets went out and you had to have your sulfur and molasses. They tried to give it to you in a way so that by Good Friday or Easter Saturday, your system had been flushed, and you were ready to meet the Resurrection on Easter Sunday! So we went to church and the place was jampacked.

It was a little warm and I had on an all-white suit. The minister was preaching. Jesus had been taken down from the cross and laid in the tomb. The church was rocking! Then the angel rolled the rock away from the tomb, and I kept pulling on Momma. She just looked at me. She's not gonna move now, 'cause Jesus has to get up out of this tomb, and the preacher is wailing "He rose!" and he rose, and he rose, and I let go! I got news for you, they had to take the collection up outside of Church.

Momma said, "I'm gonna kill you." I said, "Well Momma, I tried to tell you I had to go to the bathroom, I tried." She said, "That's too bad you tried, you didn't try hard enough." I was grounded for three weeks. I said, "Momma, I couldn't help it — you gave me that stuff." She said, "Shut up boy, don't you dare ever talk back to me." She wore diamonds and wedding rings and when one of them girls would give you a backhand lick, your lips crawled inside your throat and it would take a chisel to unwrap your lips from underneath your teeth. When they hit you, you better not cry. You moaned for the next two weeks. But I'm glad I went through all that, it made a gentleman out of me. Today they would probably call that child abuse.

I only cursed once in front of my mother and I'll tell you what happened. This ain't no lie, either. I'd just come home from the service and I thought I was bad. Momma fixed this breakfast and I said, "Oh, pass me the damn sugar." She was getting on my nerves. But she passed the sugar. She picked up the sugar bowl, and hit me right dead in the head. She said "Boy, don't you ever..." That ain't no lie. I get a headache every now and then and when I do I look to heaven and say, "Momma, you done started that crap again." I got a bump where she hit me. It's kind of gone down. I thought she was Valenzuela with the Dodgers. She hit me dead here and then I started crying, "Oh Momma!" Here I am a grown man. "Momma, why'd you hit me like that for?" She stopped that wailing right quick with "Don't you ever!"

In junior high school there was a certain amount of preparation in drama. Mrs. Thompson, the drama teacher, used to have productions like *Penrod* or other top rate productions. The auditorium would be packed for four or five nights and there would always be a great senior play. There was competition in the arts and the glee clubs were competitive through the city. The school system kept you kind of busy.

One of the big days of the year was the Sunday school picnic in Pasadena, sponsored by the black churches of Los Angeles. In Pasadena they only allowed blacks to swim at this pool once a year. For two weeks after we had our day, they'd scrub that pool. Black people carry disease, you know! Now on Easter Sunday, all the kids went to Lincoln Park where they had the scenic zoo. Studios used to shoot a lot of jungle pictures at that zoo. Those were the big, big days, Easter Sunday and going to Brookside Park. In Pasadena the residents didn't want colored people to walk down Colorado Boulevard, and you didn't go to no shows. If you did, they very obviously told you to sit in the balcony.

There was no prejudice in any of the schools. Jefferson High was an all-white school and the few blacks that moved into that territory began to go to school there with no problems. Manual Arts was all-white. I went to Washington Street School on the west side, and there were only three blacks the whole entire time I was there, from the first grade to the sixth grade. Blacks were a very small community; there was no problem, as far as the public schools were concerned.

People didn't have to look around and say this school is better for my child as a black child, because nine-tenths of the schools were ninety-nine percent white. Tom Bradley and I went to Polytechnic High School together at the same time. There were ten colored students on campus. We had our little perch where we would gather our guests, and yes, there was a certain amount of separatism at that time. We found no reason to want to hobnob with the white students.

The only thing we really wanted was to shine out in class. If you didn't shine out in class you got shined out at home. Parents of that particular era were very much interested in all the school activities. I used to regret the day I would see my mother walking into the classroom; even in my elementary school days. I knew something was up, and that I was going to catch hell when I got home. I once took an "F" grade and changed it into an "A." My mother knew. I can see her at school now shaking her head in disgust. My mother wanted to take me home right then and there. The English teacher, Mrs. Spencer, was wonderful. She knew I was going to catch hell, so she said to my mother, "Wendell has to stay until three o'clock," which would let Momma cool down.

As youngsters, we had a lot of friendly rivalries among ourselves in neighborhood gangs. I remember the Twenty-Second Street gang and the Lightning Aces. Each section of the city had gangs then. But it wasn't like it is now, with people out to kill each other. Everybody had their territory, just like they do now. Strangely, a lot of the gangs developed into the top leading social clubs of the city. The Lightning Aces became the Social Knights, the Twenty-Second Street Playground gang became something else .

Even though we had gangs, our families kept us in check. All the gangs would meet up on Halloween night, coming across the playground towards the bonfire. We made our entrance with chains and paraphernalia hanging from our pockets with our draped pants and cuffs. Not far behind would be the men folks. They stayed off in the distance, just to be sure nothing got out of hand. We didn't have any problems, we would have a tug of war, push and shove; it was typical boys and girls of that particular time.

Many of the parents would come to the bonfire, we'd have wieners and that sort of thing. That was the annual Halloween community event.

Camp was a required must. Every year for two weeks I went to camp, up in the Angeles Crest National Forest, which was organized by the YMCA. We weren't allowed to go to the downtown Y, but we really didn't care. We had our own Y which was on Ninth Street in an integrated neighborhood — but blacks built it. It was a good thing because your parents got you out of their hair for a good two or three weeks, so they could do what they wanted to do, and they knew you were under good supervision. They'd come up on Sunday of the second weekend and then there would be a big family dinner and a bonfire. Then we would all sit around and sing, so it was a bonding that took place among the parent and the child, too.

All of our parents encouraged us if we wanted to decorate or be creative. I can see Jim Franklin with a hammer and nail, helping me build a playhouse. He died when I was thirteen, and I felt all life had left me, because Jim Franklin was a real father. We'd sit down and talk, and he talked to me like a grown man about responsibility and things you had to do in life. He made sure I knew that someday I was going to have to be independent of my parents and that I'd have to make it on my own. I had to learn a certain amount of financial independence at an early age.

I always had a bank account. When I was in the third grade, everybody had to save up a dollar in pennies, then the whole class had to walk from Budlong and Washington down to the California Bank at Vermont and Washington to open a savings account. We opened it with one dollar in our book, and we got a little bank to put our pennies in. We were taught in school to save.

As a teenager, I was taught that I first had to bring my money home from all my little jobs. The family would gather and lay out all the bills for the month. My father would say, "Now, you've got twenty dollars. Your part for the month will be a dollar on the light bill, a dollar on the gas bill, two dollars on the food bill and you owe me three dollars, period." I had made money so I had to put a percentage in. I was a part of the family, I even used to do the books. Now of what I had left, I had to put seventy-five percent in the bank. The rest was my throw-away money, and I still had more than some of the kids who were doing the same thing, newspaper routes.

I remember the horse and buggy days, and rags, bottles and sacks. I saved newspapers and rags and bottles so that I could make four or five bucks every month. Then we used to steal milk bottles, 'cause you could get three or four cents off a milk bottle, when you carried it back to the store. That's when you had cream on the top of the bottle. If somebody put out their empty bottles for the milk man, I got news for you, be careful where you put them out! Kids would steal them in a minute.

I washed windows all up and down the block, to get to the Olympics Games in Los Angeles in 1932. I'll never forget when I saw Eddie Tolan and Jesse Owens run, it was one of the great moments of my life. My ticket for the relays was four and a half dollars, but I was washing windows at ten cents a piece, and that was money in those days. Regardless of what my parents could give me, I still had to learn self sufficiency and that was taught at home.

One day my mother told me that she was going to buy a top coat for me. I wanted a camel hair coat so bad, the kind with the swagger sleeves. It was fifty dollars and I knew Momma was going to get me a coat for twenty-five dollars. Don't you know, I saved up enough to buy that coat! I think this drive and sense of incentive was something that had to do with kids of that era, be they black or white. It was a means of sustaining pride within yourself.

There was a great deal of pride and self-esteem that was built-in and mostly all the kids who came up through my period have all been successful, whatever field they entered. Besides Tom Bradley, I went to school with the Knickerson kids, whose family were the founders of the Golden State Life Insurance Company. I was in class with the late Jessie Mae Beavers, who was the Society Editor of *The Sentinel*. Gertrude Gibson was a couple of years behind me, but her sister and I were in a couple of the same classes together. She was married to J.T. Gibson, the protégé of Louis Armstrong, one of the world's most fabulous trumpeters. Most of the kids I grew up with turned out to be business people, they didn't know anything about moving pictures and they weren't celebrity conscious. Many kids then were aspiring to be architects, engineers and business people. It sounds really bourgeois I guess, but everybody I went to school with, they became newspaper men, teachers, and principals. I was the only one who was crazy.

At the DGA 50th Anniversary opening ceremonies, I was standing with Arthur Hiller and Robert Wise when Tom Bradley began to speak to the packed council chamber. He said "There is one person here I've got to introduce to everybody. Wendell, come on up here. The two of us thought we were both crazy, Wendell dreamed that he was going to be a big man in film and I dreamed I was going to be a big man in government. Everybody said we were the two damnedest fools that ever went to high school."

Every parent made sure that their children went to college, just like mine did. There was a pride, you could call it bourgeois. I think a little bourgeois would help a lot of people these days.

As kids, we had seen liquor around the house, and we heard about its evils in church, and there was no way you could drink or you would go straight to hell! I remember in our big dining room we had a big side board and it was always stocked. We were allowed to have a little glass of eggnog on the holiday. It was no big thing to have liquor in the house. It was just something that never fazed us. The thing is this, anytime you got ill, you got in the bed and put three or four blankets on you and took brandy and hot lemonade; you don't need no doctor; that was the way them old girls did it! I would always see my grandmother taking a shot and she would say, "This is just for medicinal purposes." Praise the Lord! But I could see

Grandma right now, coughing, "Huummm, I feel a little cold coming down." I told her one day, "Grandma, it's a wonder you're not dead now, you've got a cold everyday." She just looked at me. That's all she had to do, I shut up.

We were naive at that time, because the world was naive. We eventually came into the drinking stage around high school, because Prohibition was finished when Roosevelt came in.

When we got a little older in high school we would go out to a party. That's when you bought liquor in the half gallons and it was the very best scotch and bourbon, 100 proof. I would steal a half pint from home and take it to the party, then I would let the fellows know how together I was. I'd lean back up at the punch bowl and there'd be twenty gallons of punch with one pint of whiskey, but fifty people got drunk. We thought that was very risqué, you know.

Our home could entertain as many as 55 to 75 people, that's when you had the big living rooms. For my wedding supper, my dining room sat one of those big long tables with all the leaves in it. We could seat forty people comfortably in our dining room. In those days women were into silver and china. The white folks had so much of the stuff in their homes that when they had parties some of them grandmothers took some home on the street cars with them. They did all the buying; they bought two pounds of butter for the madam and they went home with a pound of butter. But they weren't stealing—no way! The Lord gave this to me, child! So many homes got a full set of china which these women would bring back plate by plate. Their employers had so much in the twenties, by way of dishes and silverware that they didn't know what they had. Wedgwood and Limoges and silver. A woman's social position was determined at that time by her table linens and how she could set a table in full service. Now blacks knew service, because they had worked in these kitchens. Many a graduate from Howard University must thank his mother or his grandmother who worked in these kitchens. It was the reason why we had the money to go to college.

At that time, you sure couldn't get a job in the post office, and you could certainly forget about the fire department! We had one or two policemen on the block who were black; and then one or two on the vice squad. We didn't have any people in City Hall at all. Black people were working as waiters, chauffeurs, butlers, and cooks in the mansions of the nation. That's why we knew so much about Mr. Charlie's business, but now we've lost that underground chain. We knew what was going on, because we could hear it being discussed; we knew all about the business deals, both pending and sealed. I heard about one instance in the forties, a maid of one of the top stars built a home out in South Los Angeles and she duplicated this star's bedroom. She had the same decorator, the same bed, the same draperies and everything else. So she had this open house, and she invited her employer. This star walked in and saw her whole bedroom; she fired that black woman the next day.

BLACK L.A. IN THE 20s

The twenties I remember as very elegant and glamorous days. The black community of Los Angeles was on Spring Street and on Seventh Street, Fifth Street; the furthest we had gotten to was Central Avenue at this point, maybe at around Ninth Street, going slowly toward Twelfth Street. From Twelfth on out to Slauson Avenue was all-white — all-white. All the east side was all-white. Los Angeles was a lazy, laid back town almost like country. Orange Street used to go right up into the fields.

At that time the black community was relatively small. People had migrated here from the South. Many people from New Orleans settled here, we had a big colony of Creoles in Venice at the beach. One of the founding families of the Venice area was a family by the name of the Tabors. Los Angeles itself had its affluent Negroes — people who had worked on the railroad or in service for some of the millionaire families on West Adams Boulevard. In the early twenties, there was no Beverly Hills. All the millionaires were on Adams Boulevard anywhere from Maple and Figueroa clear out to La Brea; from there on out was oilfields, period. This was the day when ice was home delivered and men sold vegetables on horse-pulled wagons. You used to go right out the door and buy vegetables right off the street.

The black community was involved in lodges — the Masons, the Eastern Stars, the Knights and Daughters of Tabor — and churches. There were eight in town, including the African Methodist Episcopal Church. The AME Church is now a historic site, the first black church established in the city of Los Angeles, on Eighth Street. Wesley Chapel was a block or so away on San Julian just above the AME Church. Second Baptist Church was off Ninth Street, there was the People's Independent Church of Christ at 18th and Paloma, and the New Hope. These are the founding churches of Los Angeles. The NAACP and the Urban League were growing organizations which were a part of black life and culture. They used to meet on Sunday afternoons in each of the churches.

The black community was merely beginning to expand. The first black California newspaper was *The Dispatch*, owned by Frederick Madison Roberts, our first black assemblyman in the Sacramento legislature, and president of A.J. Roberts Sons & Co. He had a funeral home and a beautiful mansion at Pico and Central.

Then Charlotta Bass became the publisher of *The Eagle*, along with her husband. She became very identified with Paul Robeson and the Communist Party in the early years of the thirties; so they say.

Other big black papers that were distributed here on the Pacific Coast were *The Pittsburgh Courier*, which had seven editions out of the East, *The Chicago Defender*, *The Amsterdam News* out of New York. Then eventually there came *The Los Angeles Sentinel* from Leon Washington and that's the last of the major newspapers that we have here on the Coast now, other than San Francisco; I forgot Dr. Goodlick's paper up there. *The Sentinel* has been the stronghold here, other than the giveaway papers that are in the black areas that are owned by white companies, like *The Wave* and *Scoop*, one of the Central Avenue throwaways that has always been in the clubs and the bars.

The whole city block of Spring Street between Third and Fourth bounded by Main was owned by a single black woman, Libby Owens. She was a midwife to all the whites. All the rich whites of society of that time were living on Bunker Hill, it used to be gorgeous with all the mid-Victorian homes. The Mason Opera House was located in that community and eventually the Los Angeles Philharmonic Auditorium was situated there along with the Biltmore Theater. The Mayans and the Belascos were among the white millionaire society that lived on Bunker Hill. The Hill later fell into deterioration, but much of it has been redeveloped now.

I don't think anybody was particularly concerned about prejudice in the twenties in Los Angeles, but of course, there were lynchings going on all over the country. Glendale, a little suburban community north of the city, was known for its racism, and travel to Burbank for people of color was a no-no. When you went through the city of Compton, there used to be a sign that said, "Read and Run," meaning "Nigger keep going." In its early years, Compton was a very affluent white community.

We had a different kind of prejudice. I'll call it "California Prejudice," because every region of the country had its different degrees of prejudice and racism; prejudice in the South was different than in New York and Chicago. But prejudice in Los Angeles was strange in a way.

You couldn't eat in the restaurants in Los Angeles proper; eating at the Brown Derby and all these places, that came many, many years later. At the Ambassador Hotel, you worked there and you used the back door to go into the hotel. But the point is this, nobody really cared about it. Blacks were building lovely homes. You could build a five bedroom home and have property for ten thousand dollars. Some of these same houses now cost three hundred thousand dollars. It was a different type of lifestyle and attitude then. Blacks were very interested in enterprise and eventually they would set up one of the first insurance companies of America, the Golden State Life Insurance Company. We had our own world, Mary McLeod Bethune was coming up on the horizon along with Mary Church Terrell.

Going out to the beach in the twenties and thirties was like going to Disneyland today. Santa Monica had the big pier and the roller coaster. Venice and Santa Monica were the same place then, it didn't make any difference. Blacks never lived down on the beach front. They lived up in the city. We never talked about Venice or Santa Monica, we only called it the beach, because that was the only part of it we could go to.

Whites were living out there and blacks went out there to service them, some settling there. You had the Red Cars to travel by, they were the finest cars that we ever had in Los Angeles. The tracks are still visible on some of the streets in Venice. The Red Cars used to run all the way from Fifth and Hill straight out to the beach, great big red cars that were connected to each other and looked like trains.

The fare was five cents. Blacks would take these Red Cars and come out to the beach. At Santa Monica beach right where the Jonathan Club was, we had what was called the "Inkwell," the part of the beach reserved for blacks only. We were not allowed to swim the whole rest of that Pacific Ocean. The "Inkwell" was probably a half block wide.

Families would have big picnics there. At that time all the black people in Los Angeles knew each other. All the old families kept a kinship among them. If you didn't see people during the week, on the summer weekends everybody you knew in Los Angeles was at the Inkwell.

Down here at Venice and Santa Monica was where they used to have the black minstrel shows, on the pier. You paid to go in and there would be a black group, Mr. Bones and Mr. Ham. Kids today would very much resent it, but that's the way it was then and it was accepted by black society. It was a part of their culture at that particular time.

I hear people talking about the negative image of the mammies in motion pictures. Those women and men who played the mammies, the maids, the cooks and the butlers were the forerunners to the Sidney Poitiers, the Harry Belafontes, and the Cicely Tysons of today. Many people talk about how derogatory Lincoln Perry (Stepin Fetchit) was for the black image. I think he was a satirist who really made mockery of what the white man thought he was, with him scratching his head and rolling his eyes, because Lincoln Perry was a very articulate man.

At one time in motion pictures, anything black was black paint. Even in the late sixties at Universal, when they needed a double for a black actor, they took a white stunt man and blacked him up, because we had no black stunt men at that time.

Most of the time, these minstrel shows came into a big vacant lot in your business area and that's where you saw them. Out of these events grew the gospel tents or "chautaquas." That was a very important era in black life. It was the advent of vaudeville and many of our artists started in the minstrel shows, which were an important part of black culture in the twenties. They established a tradition. I think it stems all the way from the plantation when on Saturday nights, field hands used to put on entertainment in the cotton field for their fellow slaves. Later on, folks would have to put on shows for the people at the big house — their masters.

A. C. Harris Bilbrew used to put on one of the biggest shows in L.A. in the twenties, "The Ladies Minstrels." She was one of the women who I was really inspired by. She was a part of the first black all-talking motion picture, made by Fox in 1929, *Hearts in Dixie,* with Eugene Jackson, Bernice Pilot and Richard Carlyle, and Madame Sul-Te-Wan. All the ladies of the community would get together and stage a show at the Philharmonic. It was one of the premiere events of Los Angeles society at the time. The church was the platform for plays and operettas, and this was an early opportunity for me to be involved in putting on programs. Fortunately, the Independent Church was one of the most liberal churches. We used to have movies, the latest films, on Sundays nights at our church and it would be packed, you couldn't get in. All the other ministers raised Cain, because Independent Church had the most controversial policies.

Doctor Napoleon Greggs, my godfather and pastor of the church, believed that young people should dance, so we put on a show with the Bennett Sisters, Constance and

Joan. They did a fundraiser for us, dancing right on the church rostrum for days. We didn't have all this superstition. You go to some churches now, and you can't cross the pulpit, because this is holy-holy ground. It ain't nothing but wood and carpet.

For blacks in the twenties, there was a grandness. Those who worked in service never took Thursday off, they took off Friday so they could simulate some degree of status. People became very conscious of who was off on Thursday and who was off on Friday. On Friday and Saturday, they had what they called "breakfast clubs" and I can still see these beautiful black ladies in their wonderful touring cars, the Studebaker and the Grand Page. One of the pillars of black society, Nellie Conner, even had a Rolls Royce. At that particular time, they didn't want to sell Cadillacs to blacks. The top car you got was a Ford or a Buick. Only the funeral homes had Rolls Royces with the big headlights and I thought they were the most beautiful cars. At times, the Friday morning breakfast club would meet at our house. All these women would line up in front of our house; these women were the strength of the community, along with their men.

CENTRAL AVENUE IN THE 30s

It was a big day when you got on the Red Car and came out to Hollywood Boulevard to Grauman's Chinese Theater. The theater was a fabulous place with all the personnel being Japanese and Chinese, with beautiful robes and costumes, and the building done in grand period style.

Down the street was the Egyptian Theater which was fantastic and had the full court like a fortress in Arabia; all the guards would walk across the building with their muskets and their beautiful Arabian costuming. This was when Hollywood was Hollywood, when it was truly glamorous. Fortunately, I saw this particular era.

Then suddenly came the Big Crash of 1929. Overnight, everybody lost everything. People were jumping out of buildings killing themselves. In the twenties everybody thought that the money was going to last forever. Everybody looked like they were rich. A dollar was worth a dollar. You could get a Cadillac for two thousand dollars at the tops for the biggest car in the world. The Ford was selling for five hundred dollars. Then all of a sudden all this was gone. I guess it affected me somewhat because I had been accustomed to a certain lifestyle before then.

When the Depression hit, I was thirteen or fourteen years old, but it was a hell of a thing. I saw people in the streets crying. People's homes were gone. Banks were closed; you couldn't get your money out of the bank. The world went dark.

It was the strangest thing; the entertainment business survived because everybody needed some form of escapism. Around the time of the crash, sound came to the movies in 1929. We would see some of the motion picture companies shooting down on the railroad tracks along Alameda. They used the station at 103rd Street where the local Red Cars stopped for the people who were living out in Watts. Watts started at 103rd Street and then went to 116th Street to Willowbrook, which was all solid black.

Watts was designed to be a black community, a settlement of blacks maybe three blocks long. My family opened up a grocery store and a butcher shop on 111th and Compton. There were only three or four black kids that lived in the Watts area that went to school there. I went to 103rd Street School, the only school in Watts, for a semester while the family was establishing the grocery store.

There were no Hispanics living there at the time and whites were moving out. It was a settlement that was supposed to be all black businesses that would be supported by a community that lived there. The Water Works was owned by blacks, at 116th Street, it was called the Pembrooke Water Works. They had the water well on their property, so that water was piped into all the homes in that area. At that time they put cesspools in, they didn't have the sewer system like they have now. There were no streets, no paved roads or whatever. When it rained, it rained, and you needed a rowboat.

The Depression began to bring about a change in the Los Angeles population. It seems as though the depression hit very hard in the South and in Texas, and more blacks began to migrate to Los Angeles from there in the late twenties. Due to this, expansion started in the Central Avenue area. Ninth Street and then Twelfth Street, Pico then to Fourteen Street and then to Washington Boulevard. It just began to look like a graph that you could see blacks spreading up across the city. Also they were expanding over to the right and left of Central Avenue towards Compton Avenue and on the other side they were expanding to Paloma and Griffith Avenue and Stanford Avenue. Past Stanford there was a white borderline again. Now with the expansion there was no question of blockbusting at this time. Whites just moved out because they were beginning to move. Some were going into the valley which was farming country. In the late twenties and early thirties, Burbank and most of the towns that have now sprung up in the valley, like Encino, were farming areas. Some were almost wild desert country.

In the meantime, the Somerville Hotel had turned into the famous Dunbar Hotel. It had been built by Dr. and Mrs. John Somerville. When it was first built in 1928, everyone thought, "This was *way* out! Forty-second and Central Avenue! Good Lord, that was way out of town, that was really in the white folks' neighborhood."

Jack Johnson the boxer, the famed "Great White Hope," put a nightclub called "The Showboat Cafe" in the other end of the hotel. Next to that was the building where the "Club Alabam" was and "The Apex Breakfast Club" was above it. There was the famous Hummingbird Cafe, on Twelfth Street, owned by a Doctor Nelson.

Now these clubs were primarily designed for the white folks, just like the Cotton Club in Harlem. Black folks didn't go to the Cotton Club, it was designed for the white folks. The carbon copy of the Cotton Club out here was the Sebastian Cotton Club in Culver City.

The whites were pleasure seekers, it was very much the "in" thing to go over to the East Side. It was very chic among the movie stars and white society members to go to a club that had all black entertainers and black waiters, but it wasn't called slumming in those days. They used to have the blues singer walk around and lift the money off the table. Those things you saw in *Lady Sings the Blues* were true. Even in the thirties with the Depression, a certain amount of the twenties values and styles still existed. Women still bobbed their hair, and I remember as a little kid, when a woman cut her hair it was considered scandalous. A woman was noted for her virginity by the length of her hair.

The Somerville family went out of business and the hotel remained closed for a long time. They tried to get my family interested in taking over the hotel, but they didn't want it. So the hotel became the Dunbar, named after the poet Paul Laurence Dunbar. Seventh Street was all gone by then, it was all wiped out. It had been the crux of the black community, but everyone moved out. *The California Eagle* was at Ninth and Central, we had our own drugstores and doctors offices at Eighteenth and Central.

Personally, I think the black man fared better during the Depression than the whites. I mean we had nothing to lose, we weren't in the stock market. We had no banks of our own. There was one hospital over on 15th and Naomi, run by Dr. Stovall; it was really more like a clinic. Cedars of Lebanon was only for the stars, you didn't think about going to one of those kinds of hospitals, most people went to the County General Hospital.

At that time, they had what you called the poor folks farm, which was way out in the Valley. When you were poor, that's where you went, especially when you became of age. Nine-tenths of black people didn't put their parents in nursing homes. They used to have a screen porch or an extra room on the tail end of the house, and when they got to their seventies and eighties, that's where they were until they passed away.

In the thirties, welfare was thought of as degrading. If you mentioned anything about welfare to the average person, they would turn it down because they had pride. People did accept work like the building projects program, but it did not mean welfare because you had to work. Roosevelt established many things like the WPA, Public Works, and the Federal Theater Project. Many people were making ninety dollars a month in 1933 or 1934 and that was money, big money!

Roosevelt was our Moses. I say that because when the man died we walked in the streets in tears. With the WPA, black or white, you had a job. Regardless of your color, it went by whatever your talents were, whatever your trade was. The WPA didn't bring blacks into pictures, because Hollywood has always been a closed door. Now there are two or three windows open, but the door is still locked and all you can do is peek through the keyhole. The WPA meant work for many people, just like the National Youth Administration. Many thousands of us completed college educations with money earned in those programs. I had the chance of setting up the National Youth Administration office on the East Side when I was just a young kid, and all the staff were older than me The government furnished the typewriters and office supplies, and everybody got paid. These projects that were established through the Depression were fantastic. It was salvation. That's the reason why a lot of people holler about the Democratic party and its social programs. Roosevelt believed that if you paid a person a simple wage, that person would always want to work. I feel that those programs would benefit society today.

Black enterprising still went on, establishing funeral homes, like Connor and Johnson's, S.A. Williams, Roberts, and Angela's Funeral Home, the showplace designed by Paul Williams. Central Avenue was a showplace. Sunday afternoons when you got out of church, you would stroll down the Avenue. My church, the Independent Church of Christ, was at 18th and Paloma. At this time, all these neighborhoods were integrated among blacks and whites. Five homes would be white and then there would be a black family. All this branches off Central Avenue.

Then a few blacks began to move over on the west side, which I would say was now the elitist group, but black families had established themselves on the west side of Los Angeles back in the 1880s. My family was one, the Collins' lived off Western Avenue and the Snyders' lived on West 35th Street, which was the showplace street of black society for a block or two in there.

Back to the other side of town on East 15th Street, some of the most affluent blacks at that time were people who were into the construction business. Every piece of stone and gravel that went into City Hall was done by the Harvey Brothers, a black company. The Harvey Brothers had their own rock, ground and gravel company over by the Los Angeles River, which wasn't concrete then. They supplied the rock and gravel for City Hall. When they built this building, I remember it was like a skyscraper, it was the tallest building in Los Angeles.

The Harveys and another group of affluent blacks moved over into the West Temple district, which was considered the black Hollywood of the thirties. This is where Lincoln Perry, a.k.a. Stepin Fetchit, owned a big apartment house and was noted for his fabulous parties along with Ben Carter, who became the first black casting agent in Hollywood. Many of the blacks who had been in silent pictures and the early talkies in the thirties lived in this particular area.

So you have three different areas of affluent blacks, the West Temple District, the East Side and the West Side. However, when you got to the West Side, divisions began to come into play for the first time. We began to mimic our white brethren, arguing over who lived where and how good their home was. On West Adams Boulevard which was the peer of Los Angeles white society, the movie colony began to move in. Jack Dempsey and his wife Estelle had this gorgeous mansion on the corner of Adams and Washington Avenue, which is now a hospital. Fatty Arbuckle lived near there and the Dohenys lived at Adams and Figueroa — they built a fabulous church there. They imported the marble steps from Italy for something like fifty thousand dollars.

Then there was the Doheny mansion (Chester Place) and St. James Park. This was gate enclosed and if you pass there now, it still has a certain amount of glory to it. USC owns all of that now; it's where the Chancellor lives. This area was all the Dohenys', the Lichenbergers', but soon as the black Hollywood stars began to move into the area, the rich whites began to close their estates and they moved to San Marino. At that time, if you were in show business you were looked down upon by society, which still happens now at occasions. Top money society didn't accept show people; they were only there to entertain them.

So the likes of Mary Pickford and Douglas Fairbanks found these hills covered over with brush, which eventually became Beverly Hills. You could buy this land for a song and dance, and that's why they got these big estates built. When Pickfair was built it was surrounded by nothing but hills and brush.

Even with all of its misery and rebuilding of the American economy, the Depression had its glamour. Hollywood was the dreamspot of the world. Talkies were in, the big musicals, Busby Berkeley and the girls, it was all very glamorous. As a kid, I remember that travelling to Universal Studios was like going fifty thousand miles. You took the street car out there, but it took forever! It was a big thing in those days, just going to Warner Bros. and Paramount, just to stare at the outside gates.

Grauman's Chinese Theater used to have prologues before the picture. There would be a big production number that would feature the theme of the picture. So for *Trader Horn*, as soon as they blacked out the theater, a big stage show began with an all- black cast of "Africans" because the picture, *Trader Horn* was set in Africa. All of the blacks in the production were from around Central Avenue and they were beating drums and walking around in G-strings. Then the lights went down and the screen flashed, "TRADER HORN." Remember, this was 1931, and I was a 15-year-old kid, so this was really something, because you only got to go to the theater in Hollywood once or twice a year.

When we would go into the theater, the ushers told us the theater was full and that we had to sit upstairs on the side balconies. If you sat downstairs, they wouldn't insult you, but they tried to persuade you to do otherwise, "Would you take the balcony to the right?" You had ushers all over the place in those days, because all of these theaters were plush. Yet nine-tenths of us cared less about going to the white theaters. If Sinatra or Lionel Hampton was at the Paramount or at the Million Dollar, then blacks would try to go to those theaters.

But the black community went to its own theaters. We had at least fifteen theaters on Central Avenue and one of the last to be constructed was the Lincoln Theatre, the counterpoint to the Apollo in New York and the Regal in Chicago. Built in 1927, at 23rd and Central, it was one of the most fantastic theaters of the time.

During the thirties, black movie theaters showed black newsreels which featured Elks Conventions and beauty contests in addition to black shorts. Some pictures were made by black companies with all-black casts. I remember the Micheaux picture, *Body and Soul*, that played with a double feature. You also had black subject films, but they were made by whites. Harry Popkin, for example was a Jewish man who made a fortune in those days, he had a black version of the *The Little Rascals* which was called *The Dead End Boys*. This was done with Sheffield and Louise Beavers.

Willie Covan's nephew, DeForest Covan, who is still living, had quite a part in it. Willie Covan had this dance studio, right across from Jefferson High School, and every top star went to Willie Covan to learn how to dance. Willie Covan has never been given credit as far as I'm concerned. He trained nine-tenths of all the classic cinema stars, even Fred Astaire, Jimmy Cagney and Eleanor Powell — all of these people went to Willie Covan to learn how to tap and ballroom dance.

In cinema history, the Nicholas Brothers have never been put on the same par as Gene Kelly and the rest of them, but those are the boys that started ballet and tap dancing. I think there are so many things that have been missed on the black contribution to film. There were blacks on jungle movies where they were supposed to be savages. Now blacks aren't generally savages, they had to act in these parts, but it wasn't recognized as acting by the white directors, they were just acting "naturally." They had an African consultant who was Madame Sul-Te-Wan's son, I forget his name. He was consultant for all the *Ooba Gooba* pictures. All of those people were from the Los Angeles black community. There was a bus that would come down to Central Avenue and for maybe five dollars a day, you went to the studio, got "nekkid" and put on your G-string and became African for the then-popular Tarzan and other jungle pictures.

Everybody worked as an extra. Hollywood! They used to have buses on Sunset Boulevard that took you to the studios; if you wanted to be in pictures it was no big thing and you got three dollars for it. White folks would have a dress call for evening wear; they'd bring their own tuxedo and I think they would get three dollars more for that. I remember when you could get five dollars and if somebody got you the job, you had to give them fifty cents for that. It was a big thing. People would go through the neighborhood saying "Hey, there's an extra call today! I'll meet you on the Avenue, the bus will be at Forty-second and Central."

It was while working as an extra on the set of *Rainbow on the River* that I saw Nina Mae McKinney, at Universal in 1936. Bobby Breen was the kid star. That was the last time I saw Nina until I came home from the service on leave and I gave a party. A guest brought her to the party, but nothing was happening for her then. She outdid her own self, but in that particular period, if you was light, you was right for Hollywood standards.

I remember the first time I saw Nina Mae. I was walking up to Seventh Street, in September 1929. I was still in junior high school. I saw this gorgeous black woman all in white furs, with these white poodles, being driven up in this big Rolls Royce, a red carpet affair. At that time, in Los Angeles, the Broadway was *the* cinema of the movie houses. They refurbished the Palace Theater for her premiere. She was only sixteen at that time.

The first live drama I ever saw was performed by the Lafayette Players, a resident repertory theater that came out here from New York. But here was Evelyn Preer, Edward Thompson, Cleo Desmond, and Clarence Muse. I mean you're talking about theater! They opened with *Rain*. The Lafayette Players did everything that was on Broadway. *Rain* was a white play, done by a Negro cast. They didn't necessarily have to do a black play because they were black people — drama is drama.

The Lafayette Players were famous throughout America. Evelyn Preer was a fantastic actress. A number of years later, I studied theater under Cleo Desmond.

Clarence Muse got his start with the Lafayette Players, and I remember him best in *The Cat and the Canary*, which was later made into a motion picture. All of these plays were the same works that the white folks were doing. The Lafayette Players didn't necessarily do *Uncle Tom's Cabin* or black liberation. They did plays like *Emperor Jones*, which Paul Robeson later made famous in motion pictures. The average actor in theater and the motion picture actor were two different people. There was the thespian, and then there was the movie actor and actress.

The Lincoln Theatre was in a white neighborhood. When I say white folks neighborhood, I only think of it now as that, because as a kid, it was just people who lived there as far as I was concerned. All of our neighbors were white, they were Jewish and German, they were the Wanamakers, the founders of Thrifty's Drugstores and were some of the leading lawyers of this city. As kids, we all went to school together. A Japanese family, the Sichimodos lived on the corner of 22nd and Vermont, and they owned a nursery that covered a whole city block. As a youth, my "hang out" gang was black, Japanese, German, and French; come to think of it, there were no Southern whites that lived on our block. They went into Glendale, Burbank, Long Beach, and other outlying areas.

Central Avenue was the mainstream of all black life. I guess what Wilshire Boulevard means to a lot of people, Central Avenue meant to my generation. The Dunbar was the mecca for all the top black people in America. The Lincoln Theatre was the top mecca for all the stars of the theater; Peg Leg Bates, Broomfield and Greeley, and Bilo and Ashes, who were one of the top comedy teams of the time. Big shows were also staged at the Cotton Club where there would be a chorus line of thirty girls on the stage.

There was a show called *Central Avenue* that depicted all of Central Avenue life and I don't know whatever happened to that script, but now nobody can find it. The stars of those days were Clarence Muse, Louise Beavers, Hattie McDaniel, Lincoln Perry, Bill Robinson, Eddie "Rochester" Anderson. All of those people were part of the Central Avenue scene. I used to hear about Central Avenue and people put it down in a very mysterious way, but it was a part of black history in Los Angeles. We don't like to talk about all phases of Central Avenue, but it was like any other neighborhood. Here were your beauty shops, pool rooms, clubs, theaters, and churches; I don't care what it was, it was there on Central Avenue.

When a white company called Eastern Columbia Furniture first located on Central Avenue, they did so because they knew that it was a good market for blacks to buy furniture, rather than having them go downtown to the good furniture stores. At that time Washington Boulevard was funeral row. I remember this because it was the first time that a friend of mine was buried by a white funeral home. I was shook, because there was no way in those times. You had your own businesses then. You cared less about wanting to go to the man, you see.

The heyday of Central Avenue and the East Side was during World War II, when people came out here from the South and all over the world to work in the shipyards and the airplane plants. That's the thing that brought Los Angeles from a town to its growth into a city. Little Tokyo was about two blocks, the barrios where the Hispanics are all now was all Jewish. Brooklyn Avenue, Evergreen,

Evergreen Cemetery that was all Jewish country. From Washington and Central and as far east as you could go was white. As you got further South it was the poorer whites.

Washington Boulevard just off of Central Avenue was where the elite set resided, the doctors and the lawyers with their big homes with the front porches. That was another wonderful era of people sitting on their front porch and everybody being neighborly. The grand people separated themselves, they moved on the other side of town to the west side.

There was a color line. The Episcopalian Church with Father Claighorn was all of a light hue; the Methodist and the Baptists were a range of different types of educational levels and skin colors. Then there was the Church of God in Christ, the Holiness Church, which was established in 1921 by Bishop Crouch, that was altogether another group of religious people. Then there was the Catholic Church right off of Central Avenue and Clinton, no blacks went out to Jefferson and Central Avenue to the Catholic Church, I think that it is called Holy Name; that was very rare, I mean you weren't even in the church then. In the Catholic Church and most of the white churches at the time, blacks didn't do anything but vacuum the rugs. Everybody goes to church together now.

In those days, the minister was a college-educated man. Most of the black ministers went to Fisk University. They all had degrees in theology—T.L. Griffith, Reverend Lively, Reverend Dean and Dr. Greggs—all men of the cloth in Los Angeles. They were fluent in the classics, languages like Latin and Greek. There weren't these instant ministers like "God spoke to me last night and told me to take up the cross." These men were trained as administrators and businessmen and most of all, they were trained to be community-minded.

Everybody and his brother got up in church on Sunday and recited Paul Laurence Dunbar. "Come hea' chile, we gonna get some cornbread." The black church was not just a preaching haven, we also heard all the black poets and important practitioners of black culture. I remember saying to my school chums, "Where can I get a copy of that Langston Hughes poem, I want to memorize it." I read Booker T. Washington, and *The Souls of Black Folk* by W.E.B. DuBois, which I read when I was nine years old. Those books were in our home.

I think there was a lot of progress in those days, maybe even more than now. Writers then weren't necessarily considered black writers. They were considered writers, and they happened to be black. Langston Hughes' poetry writing was read by the world.

The church of that day was the primary instrument that helped set up the insurance companies, helped set up the businesses. The minister would tell his congregation, "Go and patronize that man or person." Ministers would stress the importance of improving your property and keeping your yard clean, but I don't hear that anymore. All I hear now is about money grabbing, but people in those days built beautiful churches and money had a different value then.

After church got out, you promenaded down Central Avenue. I mean you fell out in your best clothes! The streets would be packed on each side of the road. "Hey there!" "Hello there," and talking about the Easter Promenade. I got news for you! That was the one thing that the black families did in those days, just like you knew for sure that every third Christmas you were going to get a new overcoat.

For Easter you had your white pants, your blue blazer coat and white flannels with the patent leather shoes. You knew you were going to get a suit, and in those days you got two pair of pants with the coat. One pair of pants you could wear to school for nice occasions and the other pair served for Sunday. Everybody had a blue serge suit, that was a requirement, period. We didn't wear blue jeans, because only people in jail wore blue jeans. Black men wouldn't have their sons running around in Levis. Corduroys were the thing.

Everybody hung out on the Avenue and this is where all the events were happening. There were places like the Masonic Lodge Hall and the Elks Auditorium, a beautiful three-story building with a huge ballroom. Another activity was the girls' reserve from the Y, where we used to have matinee dances on Saturday afternoon. I mean you got dressed on Saturday morning to make it to the afternoon matinee dance, where all the young people gathered. Back then, we always had some place to go. I belonged to two or three social clubs, including the Junior Elks and the Gimpers.

A lot of kids' parents didn't allow them to go to dances until they were 18 years old. A young lady then didn't flaunt around till she was 18 or 19. It was the same way with the boys, but they were allowed more leeway because they were men. Most of the young ladies were presented with a party at home in the backyard or a debutante ball to acknowledge that they were eighteen. That was done by every family regardless of their economics. A young lady's first pair of heels, her first pair of silk stockings, were something to talk about, especially the ones with the crooked seams.

FROM MINISTRY TO MARRIAGE

When I finished high school in the mid 1930s, my family felt the idea of a career in motion pictures was very remote at that time. The people in the black world were real estate people, ministers, doctors, lawyers, dentists, and mailmen. There were only a few that were in the post office at this time. There were no blacks at this time in the fire department in Los Angeles. Besides working in service, restaurants or local community businesses, there weren't too many opportunities for blacks. Being very much involved in the Church, which was the center of black life, everybody predicted that I was going to go into the ministry. I was very sincere about it at this point, so I enrolled in the Los Angeles Theological Seminary.

With the backing of the family, I started studying theology, but I saw that this was not going to work with me. I was looking at it purely from the standpoint of prestige, not from the sincerity of winning people for heaven. I dropped out in the first year. I had planned to go to the University of Southern California (USC), but the school at the time was a very prejudiced one.

I got involved in doing some shows with Joe Adams of KDAY, who was the first top black disc jockey here in Santa Monica. He had met Walter Winchell at the Club Alabam. The Damon Runyon Cancer Fund was the popular charity at the time for entertainment people. Nothing had been done in the black community in Los Angeles. I got together with Joe Adams, Edward (Deeson) the leading cosmetologist and beautician in this city, and his business partner Frank Jackson. Joe, who had all the connections said, "Why don't we put on a show for the Damon Runyon Memorial Fund for Cancer Research and have Walter Winchell as the chairman?" On our own, we raised about five hundred dollars and rented the Philharmonic Auditorium. We put a cast together of Lionel Hampton, the Hall Johnson Choir, Redd Foxx, and Benny Carter; all the musicians in the union donated their time.

We had enough show to run for three hours. It was the tops in entertainment. We didn't sell out the Philharmonic but we didn't do too bad either. I modeled the show using nothing but drapes and hung curtains that were donated to me by scenic companies. Even the bandstand and risers were donated. We just went out and begged; it was for the Damon Runyon Memorial Cancer Fund and you couldn't turn that down, because Winchell would say something about it in his column. Walter Winchell was bigger than Hedda Hopper and Louella Parsons. He was one of the biggest men in America, and all you had to do was mention Walter Winchell's name and the doors opened. That's the reason why I always say why go to the son when you can go to the father. Why go to Jesus when I can go to God? I learned that a long time ago. I've always gone to the top, I've gotten myself in trouble — but anyhow, that was a successful show.

Also during this time, Edward suggested to me that we put on a revue show of hairstyles and fashions. I was only about nineteen or twenty, but I put the show together and staged it. We did five editions of this revue, which we titled *Dreams in Silhouette.* We presented the show at the world-famous Earl Carroll's, which eventually became the Moulin Rouge. We asked all of the top young ladies of the community to be the models. One young lady, LaTanya, later became a famous designer in Europe and America. We had fabulous sets to work with, and our staging became a byword in America. We did an innovation with sixteen girls all wearing a copy of the same dress, coming down the staircase. We also used quite a few gimmicks, such as girls coming out of the ceiling and the side stages and a revolving stage. We would get a very plain looking woman from the audience and would do a makeover on her in two minutes. Edward knew how to take a roll of material and create a dress on stage. Nine gentlemen in tails escorted the women onto the stage, singing, "You're a lovely girl, you're like a beautiful melody." Another thing we did was to get shoes for twenty girls from the best shops. I would spot the light so that it would be right on their feet. The girls would unwrap their legs to the left and then to the right to show the type of shoe.

We carried this show for NAACP benefits up north in the Oakland Civic Auditorium. I went ahead of the show for a few days to look for the right scenery and props. Up there I'd have seven columns lighted from the inside to give the show a theatrical effect. When it came to the stage design, I just went by my own feelings. I always had that type of intuitiveness. The furniture changed at least once a week in my mother's house. My stepfather would complain that he could never get in the house; every time he came home, the furniture was changed. I had staged many things before that time in the church. In my church, we brought in spotlights, curtains and actors. The church trustees used to get mad at me because I wanted a very large staging area and I would fill in the pulpit with extra staging by taking out the rails and all the choir seats. I would use full curtains and electrical buttons from the balcony with full footlights and side lighting.

An interest in film and theater has always been a part of me. When I was in elementary school, *The Herald Examiner* used to advertise that if you sold ten cases of this hair dressing, you'd get a motion picture projector and some films you could grind yourself. So I sold those cans at twenty-five cents a piece, and they sent me my projector. I took one of the garages underneath one of the apartments we owned and set up a screen with curtains and seats with rows to walk down on the side and all the kids came over and paid an admission of three cents. So I had my own theater. I had a short of Charlie Chaplin and several other things.

As kids, our families would have us put on plays in the living room, we would just get a bunch of kids together and put on a little show. I've always been in some form of theater or show business. I put on a really good production at the Lindy Opera House which was at Wilshire and La Brea before they tore it down. I also staged shows and events at Ciro's and the Florentine Gardens.

Several social clubs and some of the people who organized fashion revues would get a choreographer to show them how to incorporate dance in their presentations. Many of these people were matrons and civic workers and their friends would come and watch them kick up their heels. It was a lot of fun and we always had a sellout. I would light the stage. I've always had my hands on good technicians. We took time to play with the light and to see what we could work out. One of my best friends was Lon Fontiane, who choreographed the Temptations and many other Motown groups. I helped him get a deal on *Lady Sings the Blues* as a choreographer.

I did undertake some training in little theater. Under the tutelage of Cleo Desmond of the Lafayette Players, along with other thespians of the time who were having drama schools within the community, I began to take classes. At that time it seems that all of the black people who had aspired to the theater had no training, they all had natural talent. I think I was one of the first blacks who received some formal type of training in the theater. Let me say that my academic background was of a nature that was geared into the theater. Most blacks were going to Howard University, Fisk, Mehary, Bishop and other black colleges which were big at that time. The family wanted me to go to Howard but I steered them away from that.

My mother was great friends with Mary Bethune. By this time the National Youth Administration (NYA) had already been started by President Roosevelt (FDR). Its purpose was to provide part-time jobs and loans for college students. Mary McLeod Bethune was its head, reporting to Roosevelt. She was the only one who was ever able to walk into the White House to see Roosevelt unannounced. She and Mrs. Roosevelt became great friends. Sometime in the forties, there was this big luncheon at Town and Gown on the USC campus, and as I recall there were only twenty colored students on campus. Mrs. Roosevelt was introduced first, and she in turn introduced Mary McLeod Bethune. Mrs. Bethune, and I can see her hair with that net now, and that cane, said, "It's a great pleasure to be here on the campus of the great University of Southern California, with my dear friend, Eleanor. But I got a problem, Chancellor Von Kliensman. I want to see you in your office, immediately after this luncheon. I don't understand why there are no blacks on campus sponsored by NYA, but there will be before I leave today." We got up and cheered, stood on tables and everything else. She continued, "Look, I'm representing the President, and nine-tenths of these whites are on NYA, and I don't know why there aren't any blacks here on NYA, now you and your little wealthy ass college better get cracking!" Folks then began to run on the campus.

That was an illustration of what I call affirmative action. Money does have a great deal to do with affirmative action and hiring.

When the NYA set up their program in Los Angeles, I was put in charge of the administrative office within our community. There were about thirty young people my age level who were secretaries and clerks, and we set up the first employment office in the black community, extended from the United States Employment Department. Jobs would be called in from downtown, and we would do all the preliminary interviewing. Then we would send the applicants back downtown for referral to go out on the job.

Finally, through a scholarship, sponsored by my church and NYA tuition funding, I enrolled at USC. By the time my paperwork was processed, I had decided to leave. My personality got in the way, due to racism on the campus at the time. Most blacks like Woody Strode, Kenny Washington and Tom Bradley went over to the University of California, Los Angeles (UCLA). It was *miles* out to Westwood. It's funny to think about it being miles now. I decided I just wasn't going to finish my university work, although I've been back to school every now and then, over the years. I've studied photography, radio and television in a commercial school. Like most blacks, during the period of the thirties and forties in the entertainment business, we were self taught dancers, singers, and artists. People like Hattie McDaniel, Louise Beavers and Clarence Muse were just talented people. All of our artists at this particular time in the vein of popular entertainment — Redd Foxx, Moms Mabley, Mantan Moreland, Bill Robinson, Stepin Fetchit, you name them — none of them ever went to any training schools. Paul Robeson was different because he was a graduate of Rutgers, and Marian Anderson also studied. Most of our artists, like singers and even musicians, Nat King Cole or whoever, were self taught. Some of them had basic music in high schools and possessed a natural talent.

Like the good folks used to say, "Y'all got rhythm." That was true because we came from a church whose music was rhythmic. However, even more importantly, we came from a culture of people that even in the Depression and times of lower incomes were happy people, and who in spite of all the despair, knew how to clap their hands and feel good on Saturday night. Let's go back, Scott Joplin and Duke Ellington I'm sure had very basic training, and became some of the great musicians of our time. Little Richard did the same with rock and roll; Chuck Berry, Billy Eckstine, Herb Jeffries, Lena Horne, Nina Mae McKinney, the Robbins, the Inkspots, the Mills Brothers, all these people had great intuitive talent.

The white world accepted that talent because they had to learn tap dancing from blacks. Some of the great singers from the white world will tell you that they used to sit in clubs and listen to Billie Holiday or Ella Fitzgerald to find methods of styling and shadings. They would copy this in their work and they would become a star. In the past, the film studios had schools where they trained their actors how to dance, how to walk, and how to talk. Black actors and actresses were just supposed to have natural talent.

On the night of the Academy Awards in February 1940, Hattie McDaniel became the first black performer to win an Academy Award. She took the "Best Supporting Actress" award for 1939 for her performance in *Gone With the Wind.* Hattie was invited to the studio party afterwards. Like most of the parties that you attend, they're nice to you for a while and then they go off and leave you standing in the middle of the floor.

Hattie was aware this might happen. She was a very good friend of mine and Clayton Russell and his wife, and we had already announced in our church that day that Hattie might come over after the ceremony because this was a historic occasion. She arrived about 11:30 p.m., and I have never seen so much pandemonium break loose when she walked in that door. She wore a fabulous beaded gown that reached to the floor. She had to come back to her own people to receive the accolade she deserved.

So that's what happened to Hattie. Nevertheless, her home attracted people like Joan Crawford and Bette Davis, because she loved to cook — mustard greens, ham and sow belly and all that good soul food. Her living room was always packed when she lived up on Sugar Hill.

The Franklin home was only about four blocks from the hill, straight down 22nd. But we had built that house many, many years before the prime of Sugar Hill. Mayor Cryer used to live up there and many of those people had fabulous homes. Some of those homes even had big ballrooms; it's just like what happened in the East, it was one of those places and times when blacks were making that kind of money and they wanted beautiful big homes so that's what happened. Louise Beavers, the Clarks, the Bowdins, all lived on Sugar Hill.

Sugar Hill went from Western, 22nd Street from Washington over to Adams with all those great big homes. Eddie "Rochester" Anderson's house is right off of Jefferson on the elbow and it's almost a duplicate of Jack Benny's home. Bill "Bojangles" Robinson had his house custom built over on 36th Place and Catalina. They still take tour buses past the Bill Robinson home which is right near USC, but when he bought it that neighborhood was a showplace. The heyday of Sugar Hill was during the war years, when everybody made money.

I first came in contact with the Communist Party on Sugar Hill. A fellow had a home called "Dragonwyck" where we all used to go. Anyone who went to college was involved with the Communist Party in some way, period. Youth was rebelling just like they always do. They used to have these gorgeous white girls to sic on us to get us to join, and they weren't playing, the Communist Party was strong, all over this country. When World War II broke out, everybody became patriotic and said "The hell with the Communist Party!" I never carried a card and millions of others didn't either, but we sure would go up there to the parties. But before the party was over they were trying to brainwash you about the common man and all that.

There used to be other political organizations, like the California Youth Legislature which was set up like the Senate and the House of Representatives. They would have these big meetings, and once a year they would elect people to these big offices. So we were all involved, but it was always an involvement in gorgeous homes, the right atmosphere, with the booze and white women. It seems strange, but during this period many black women did not really get too much involved in this, and the only reason the fellows were involved was because they were looking for a free piece of tail. There was only a smattering of radicals at this particular time.

The church was a very influential part of my life and at one time, as a young man of twenty, I felt that I wanted to go into the ministry. I had a chance to preach my first sermon in my family's church, People's Independent Church of Christ. It's a very historical church in Los Angeles, which many outstanding people were a part of. In the thirties, going into the forties, the church had a very large congregation of over four thousand.

My family felt that whatever I wanted to do, whether it was to be a lawyer, doctor or whatever, it was okay; but I wanted to go in the ministry. I felt the church gave a chance for a certain amount of showmanship, a chance to demonstrate your feelings and to deliver it to other people. But in the course of time, as a youth, I also wanted to experience life — I mean the clubs and the social life. I always thought that a good motion picture had a message and a sermon in itself. In the pictures I saw, the good always won out and the bad always lost in the end, and that to me was what religion was all about. You had to do good, if you did bad you would go to hell.

In order to make money I did things like any other chap of my age, I worked at the Ambassador Hotel as a shoeshine boy — I was there for one of the Academy Awards when Guy Lombardo was there with a big orchestra, down on the "casino floor" which is what they called it at the time. I shined shoes for some of the top stars and executives of that time. I worked at the Hollywood Bowl in the thirties and early forties. I was washing dishes because at that time, black caterers provided all the food at the Bowl. Mrs. Bertha Turner and all the boys and girls who had scholarship rings would be hired by her for the summer to work as waiters, dishwashers and assistant cooks. We were all around the ages of fifteen and sixteen. Now when the dining room closed and people were preparing to see the opera of the evening, I'd have all four of us in the kitchen washing dishes.

As soon as we got out we'd run up to the Bowl and there'd always be a box vacant and we'd see the show. Back then they used to have Grand Opera with all the grand staging with Max Reinhardt, and productions like *Midsummer Night's Dream.* I remember when Mickey Rooney made his debut as Puck. They used to move that shell out and build great big sets. I'll never forget seeing Aida the first time — Aida was doing this spectacular aria on the throne and her father was in the background in these great big chains. Well, this elephant just happened to have a condition occur. Plop, plop, right in the middle of her great aria and I've got news for you, the elephant's tail was just switching to the time of the music and she kept on singing!

Every now and then, I'd get a job as a houseboy. I was involved in so many things that my family pushed me for and my mother was very encouraging to me. When I was involved in community work like staging plays and fashion shows, I'd get ten or fifteen dollars and that was it, period. I never really knew what a salary was during that time.

In those days if you didn't marry by the time you were twenty-two or twenty-three, it just wasn't kosher, especially if you were a young lady. So I pursued a young lady who was from a very prominent and affluent family in Los Angeles, and we were married in 1942. From that union came a son. The strangest thing was that my mother — and all mothers know their children — sensed that married life would not work for me at this time, because I wanted a career.

I wed with the idea that it was the thing to do, not thinking about the security that marriage requires. My father-in-law got me a job at Sears and Roebuck pushing a broom, and I said to myself, No way, I'm not going to sit around and talk about how many years you would be here until you retire. That was his school of thought for his generation, and God bless him for it. I always had the dream or the fantasy that there was something better in life for me. If you never dream or fantasize, you can never make the first step toward any kind of career.

I had to grow and mature, and very soon, I decided that marriage came second to having a career. At that time in black society, the entertainment business was not thought of as a sure business and talking about film was so far fetched that really, it was a dream. I guess I ran like a coward when marriage became a closing wall on me, and enlisted in the armed services.

ARMED SERVICE

When I first shipped out of L.A. to go to Fort MacArthur, I went with my white buddy, Earl from next door. But when we got there, we were separated. This is the first time that I fully realized the impact of segregation. It was kind of traumatic to me. We would meet off the post while at Fort MacArthur, but eventually we were shipped out. I just couldn't understand why we had to be separated; Earl and I had planned to bunk together and all that. So I was shipped to Seattle, to Fort Lauten and then to Excursion Inlet.

Excursion was a secret base way up in the Pacific Northwest, near the Aleutian Islands. Almost 8,000 black men from the South had been shipped in to be dockhands, stevedores, truck drivers, and the like. I was brought in along with a group of other Californians to form a cadre company that would administrate extracurricular programs for the welfare and the well-being of these men.

All our officers were white until the tail end of the war, when a black captain was brought in. It was very much an undemocratic society between the white officers — thirty-day wonders from officer training school — and the blacks from the South. There were many fine black men who had been denied an education, but who had strong backs. The delegation of black Californians had college backgrounds and this helped them get positions in the administration.

One time around Christmas, the men's morale had become very bad — the war was at its height, and there was no mail from home since before Thanksgiving. So it was our idea to put a soldiers' show together. At first it was a no-no, but a black captain pushed it. We were able to recruit from all the port companies' talent — among that talent were songwriters, scriptwriters, men who helped make scenery. We put together a show we called *Excursion Inlet Scandals*, with a chorale group of 150. Sadly, some of our black brothers said it wasn't going to be nothing but another nigger show for the white folks, but in our hearts we knew better.

All the personnel on detached service to the cadre company rehearsed for six weeks in preparation for opening night. General Eley P. Densen, down from the Seattle Port of Embarkation, along with dignitaries from Washington, was at the post theater for our show. There was a command issued to all personnel to attend, which was not well received by some of the soldiers stationed with us. Here was a turning point in my life. What a show, what a show! I saw hundreds and hundreds of black men give that show a standing ovation. This continued for five nights. At the conclusion of the performance, General Densen said "Wendell Franklin, when you're back in the States, look me up in the office."

Well, that day wasn't too long in coming. At the base, there were a lot of living conditions that weren't healthy. When we finally got a black Brigadier General on inspection of our post, we wanted to register complaints with him. We tried to, we even went to the Colonel's living quarters to request an interview with the Brigadier General, but were refused. He claimed that everything was all right and that we should be happy. Well, by us going over the heads of our immediate commanding officers directly to the commandant of the installation, we were accused of insubordination. So we were all railroaded back to the States.

When we got off the boat we went straight to the Seattle Port of Embarkation, not on to Camp George Jordan where we were to be stationed. We went directly to General Densen's office. The General was getting on the elevator at the same time as we arrived, and I was the first one to speak up, "General Densen, when you were at Excursion Inlet, you told us to look you up in your office." He remembered and asked us, "What do you want to do?" We all agreed that we would like to follow through with entertainment activities in Seattle that would be encouraging to black soldiers who were away from home.

He offered every confidence in the world and told us not to worry about it, but on the way down from that elevator, for some reason the elevator got locked and it went back upstairs. Two lieutenants got on and they raised complete hell with us that we dare speak to the General. I told the lieutenant that we were there at the request of the General. He said "Don't you ever say that to me, you come through the command." We were all non-commissioned officers, so on our service records it was noted that we were insubordinate. Again!

We went on to Camp George Jordan and through a Captain Shelton, I rose in rank, and we were able to establish a beautiful service club and gymnasium. The fellows who were stationed there were able to form a full orchestra and a glee club, and we became the toast of Seattle. In this way, these events further encouraged my dream, since childhood, of being in the entertainment business.

Through the services I had the chance to attend Washington and Lee University. Also there were the famed musician Eddie Beale, Baxter Scruggs, who later was head of the YMCA in Los Angeles, and Reginald Arnaurd. When we got to the District of Columbia we had to change trains and it was the first time I saw this infamous little sign: "Colored people sit in the back of this sign." The Colonel in charge of our trip was incensed by this. There were state rooms on the end of each train, so rather than expose us to this subjugation, he put us in the state room at the front of the train, and in front of the whites who were riding the train. We got off at Clifton Forge, Virginia, and there was another first waiting for me. I saw a fountain that said, "For Whites Only." As soon as we arrived at Washington and Lee, we were told by a commandant that on the campus there is complete integration, but when we stepped out in the street we would be in segregated country, so we should behave accordingly.

It was one of the most beautiful campuses in America, named for George Washington and General Robert E. Lee. It had probably the greatest law school in the country, but at that time the campus had been turned into a training center for people connected with theater and motion pictures throughout the armed services. Assembled were some of the greatest minds of the arts to more or less give us a speedy education. We were to take this knowledge back to our stations to further entertainment programs for enlistees, like glee clubs and USO shows.

Well, it came time for graduation and what a graduation! All the government dignitaries were there, representing Roosevelt's cabinet. I was the only black involved in the graduation services. The big directors and producers always staged a grand, New York type show the night before graduation. A great music score had been written and they were asking for a black to audition. My friend, Eddie Beale was conducting the orchestra, which was made up of musicians who were from all over the country, top professionals. The score was written to the music of "Saint James Infirmary," which involved a chorale group backed by a full orchestra. Nobody went to the audition because there were only four of us blacks on campus and nobody thought we were capable. Eddie Beale came to me and said "Man, I don't know if you've ever sung in your life." I said "Well yes, but only in kiddy shows." He replied, "Well, you're going to sing this score." It was twenty-two pages! We did it and received a thundering, standing ovation, which was quite surprising to me; it was one of the first times in my life that I heard applause ring in my ears just for me. That was a great experience, and it entrenched me that much more in the world of entertainment.

For our graduation ball, we were once again called in by the commandant and told that we were not to dance with any of the white ladies that would be present, because there would be colored girls there who would be available to dance with us. The four of us just shrugged it off and thought, "Here we go again." Later that evening we saw this fabulous bus arrive. We saw some of the most beautiful black girls in the world get off that bus. They all had on furs and gorgeous gowns! They were students at

Vassar and Smith Colleges. Wow! They walked in and we had some of the most beautiful women I think I've ever seen in America. Even though they told us not to dance with the white girls we decided we had to go to the commandant. We told him straight, "Well if we can't dance with the white girls, then the white soldiers can't dance with the black girls." We wanted all that action to ourselves!

So this is some of the background of the prejudice that was a part of the scheme of American social life and politics at that time. I'm not the only one who went through this. I think black Americans as a whole went through the same thing, and if they say they didn't, they lied.

NBC: FROM PARKING LOT TO STAGE MANAGER

I came out of the service in 1946. I was feeling very good about myself, although I was still feeling isolated due to the prejudice and segregation within the armed services. But I was also keen to get into some activity, so with my GI Bill I enrolled at Hal Style's School of Radio and Television in Beverly Hills. As I look back on it now there were many schools in communications and TV who said that they could do everything for you. I'm sure it's a little better nowadays, but we were truly suckers back then. Beverly Hills! Television and radio! Hey, we were hot! So I studied whatever the curriculum was, and eventually got on staff at this school. I really thought I knew what it was all about.

What I really wanted to study was cinema, but there was no way. USC had a very small school, I don't think UCLA had started its film school back then. There was no way for a black to study dentistry, let alone cinema. Many of the law schools were not open to blacks at this particular time, even at UCLA and USC. Fortunately, a show came out here from New York, *Carmen Jones*, starring Muriel Rahn, with Napoleon Reed. I met Sheldon Hoskins at a party. I told him of my plight, and that I would like to go to New York to study staging. It was up to him to decide. There were four or five vacancies for dancers in the ballet of *Carmen Jones*. So they asked me to jump up and down and that sort of thing, and I didn't know my left foot from my right. Anyway, I signed a contract here in Los Angeles which I later found was always a good practice — sign before you go and get your round trip ticket in advance.

When I landed in New York, I couldn't get into the Theresa Hotel, so I stayed at the Cecil. The restrooms were down the hall. Being the simple Los Angeles yokel I was, I laid my money and my jewelry out on the dresser and went down the hall. When I got back everything was gone. Here I am in New York less than eight hours and wham! — nothing. I was scared to death to begin with. Here's the city, the Big Apple, where people push and shove and move like lightning. It had a whole different momentum and speed than I was used to. So the typical telegram went back home to Momma.

Rehearsals started at the Ziegfeld Theater — the great Ziegfeld Theater, where *Showboat* was on the tenth floor and on the main floor was William Warfield and Pearl Primus. Here was the anxiety, the push, the shove and the drive of everything that people wanted to see on Broadway. I started rehearsal in my leotard and I tried my best to skip, hop and jump, but I was a complete failure; I knew it inside of me.

The show opened out of town in New Haven, and when the trains came in the yard at 7:30 in the morning I went down to see how they unloaded all this massive scenery, and then followed them to the theater to see how they hung the set. This is what I wanted to know more about, and I knew I could not get it in any college. I wanted to see this actually happening. I watched the music conductor in the pit working with 52 musicians. Here I saw one of the most fabulous shows on Broadway that Billy Rose ever produced. I made my observations throughout the entire time I was with the company.

We got up to somewhere in Vermont, and then one of the dancers got sick and they said I had to go in. Oh, have mercy! I tried. People stumbled over me, Buck and Bubbles said "Get him off the stage!" Muriel Rahn was doing her brilliant aria from the drum dance in *Carmen* and I was about to fall into the orchestra pit. I was a klutz, but I did have the opportunity to learn a great deal of staging and how to break down a set to fit into a smaller theater. What to use and what not to.

I got fired. I went home and my mother said, "Hea, Hea, I told you so." My first week back in Los Angeles, somebody told me that NBC was hiring on the parking lot. You had to go to a certain organization — I won't name it, but you can read between the lines — which was the go-between for referring blacks to NBC. So I went to their Central Avenue office, and was told that I wasn't the type. NBC would never hire me because I wasn't the type, meaning my skin wasn't light enough.

So I called and made an appointment on my own. I got on the streetcars, and went way out to NBC. A lady by the name of Mrs. Kathryn Hardesty was head of personnel. She interviewed me and the interview was not so much about the job; it seems as though we got in a philosophical conversation about the science of the mind and rapped for an hour. The next morning I got a telegram from NBC, asking me to come to work on the parking lot. This was when NBC was at Sunset and Vine. Eventually I found out that everybody at NBC started on that parking lot or in the mail room. Stanley Robertson, who later became a Senior Vice President at NBC and Columbia Pictures, started as a page at NBC. He was the only black page at that particular time.

There were two other black fellows on the lot, which was not any old parking lot. It was by invitation only, and only the two stars could get in, and then only on the days of their show. It was up to the attendants to segregate the weep from the tears. I mean everybody was not allowed in. There was a myth that Jack Benny quit NBC because he had trouble getting on the parking lot, that's one of the stories that's always been around.

That parking lot was the holy of holies in Hollywood. By 1947, I had met every top star there has been in the entertainment world. Mary Martin, Albert McCleery with *Matinee Theater*, and Dinah Shore when she had her first 15-minute show. It was a great thrill for me. I had let Sinatra in, Sammy Davis, Jr., Judy Garland, Jane Wyman, and all the greats. Here was Hollywood in all of its essence and glory. *The Colgate Comedy Hour* was down the street where the Johnny Carson Theater is now. *Lux Radio Star Theater* was where the Doolittle Theater is now. *Queen for a Day* was across the Street at the Moulin Rouge. Vine Street was the mecca for the music recording companies.

So for ten years, I worked on the lot. I left the lot and worked for a while in the Kinescope Recording department, but soon came back to the parking lot.

Then one of the lot supervisors died and I became the supervisor; a black man in charge of one of the most prestigious parking lots in the industry. So after I became supervisor, more shows like *The Tonight Show* with Steve Allen came out from New York. Often this was done to boost the ratings of the show on the West Coast. It was then that I met Fred Lights, a very talented black man who became the first black in network stage management, and he was working on *The Tonight Show* in New York and came out to Los Angeles with it.

At this time I was pushing to be a stage manager and I knew then all the attitudes would be "Are you kidding? This is not the world for you, Wendell, you'll never make it." Well, one day when the West Coast head of RCA, which was the parent company of NBC, John K. West, came to the parking lot, I asked him if I could have an interview with him. I had been a bartender and had worked three or four parties at his home; we had developed a kind of personal relationship. So Mr. West called me up to his office in the RCA building for an interview. I was scared to death.

Here was Mr. West, all of seven feet in height, one of the top men in the industry nationally. He said, "Well, what do you want to do?" I said, "I want to be a stage manager." At least by then I put it in my head that that's what I wanted to be. He said, "Well, we'll think about it." At the annual party for the employees at the Bel Air Country Club, somebody leaked that I was going to be a stage manager, much to the disapproval of about 40 whites who had been vying for the position. Along comes this lowly black man from the parking lot, bypasses everybody else, and goes right to the stage. I followed right behind Fred Lights, being the second black stage manager in network history and the first on the Pacific coast.

The Personnel Department blew up and they were going to see to it that my appointment wouldn't happen.

They didn't succeed, and I became a stage manager on October 1, 1958. The first shows I worked on were *The George Gobel Show* and *The Eddie Fisher Show*. These shows were every other week, then when they had an extra show coming on, if you weren't doing anything they would put you on that show. Doing *The Eddie Fisher Show*, I had the chance to meet Elizabeth Taylor and she was the one who showed me how to drink bull shots and beef bouillon, of which I am very thankful that she did. Eddie Fisher was a great support in encouraging me, so was George Gobel. Dinah Shore was one of the most beautiful people I've ever met and was always very supportive of me, always telling me, "Wendell, you're going to do it."

The Nat King Cole Show was premiering then, but they couldn't even get a sponsor for Nat for six or seven months. One of the NBC executives, Hal Kemp, kept Nat on the air. Sidney Provost, the first black TV cameraman in the history of television, was on the show. Sidney got started on the parking lot, too. His father was in charge of the service department at this famous Jewish private club that Bob Burn owned, where Joe Louis was the first black to play on their golf course. It was through his father and his father's contact with John K. West that Sidney got his start. I think there was one black female crew member, a seamstress in NBC's wardrobe department.

I went to the stage much to the dismay of other people. As I look at it now, I was very inadequate, I didn't know what stage management was about. I was dumb, but I was at the right place at the right time, and asked the right questions and gave the right answers. Most of my work in the community and in little theater was directing and telling people what to do.

But as a stage manager I was cued in by the light on that camera. I had to look at this light and hear the cue from the booth, and then tell the star to speak. Sometimes my fingers would get messed up and when I should have been pointing down to the actor, I was pointing up to the camera. So, it was rather comic to a lot of other people who were willing to exploit my inexperience and inadequacies.

Rather than training me, they just said "Here you are." I think I had one day where I went down to the set to observe. One man who I can really thank is Bill Finnegan. He was a very sincere and honest person; in his limited time working from show to show, he would illustrate techniques for me and he allowed me to observe on his set. He's one of our top producers now, he worked as the producer of *Hawaii Five-0* for most of the length of the show. When the two guilds merged he was doing *The Grimm Brothers* and was the first assistant on the picture. Laurence Harvey was the star. Bill invited me out to MGM just for the day to observe. To me he was most outstanding, he was one of the first people who really was sincere in trying to help me.

Everybody else I'm sure was laughing up their coat sleeves, due to my inexperience. People wanted me to fail and they kind of paved the road if there was to be failure. Fortunately, fate has always played a great part in my life.

There were many strange things that happened. There was one particular incident I remember. The director in the booth, Barry Sheer, gave me a cue and I cued the stagehands to open the curtain. Two of them very pointedly delayed the curtain at least two minutes. Sheer was screaming at me from in the booth, because they had to go to a commercial and the commercial actors were already dancing, all hell seemed to break loose.

The point is this, I could not blame the stagehands, because you don't make up any excuses in this business, you accept the blame and get on with your job. Turning around in this business and pointing your finger at this one and that one is not going to change what happened. The white stagehands knew their cue, they just didn't like the idea of a black stage manager on the floor.

I was often made uncomfortable and found myself in some racist situations. When I was assigned to *Queen for a Day*, I watched some of the other stage managers at work to prepare for my duties on the show. When the girls were to pull back the curtains to show the gifts, the stage manager would cue them by just touching them on the shoulder. So when my turn came, I did the same thing. Jack Bailey, the host of the show, personally came back stage to cuss me out. He said "Don't you eeevverrr put a finger on a white woman." So many little incidents like this caused me to become very frustrated. That was the end of me and *Queen for a Day*.

I had eight straight working months of the stage manager position. To me they were just shows, I saw nothing that was illuminating about them, they were just popular at that time. Any encouragement for a future in the business came from people who I was associated with in television and whose shows I worked on. I had the great pleasure of working with Ralph Edwards on *This Is Your Life* and here was a man who was much of an inspiration to me. Jerry Lewis was also especially encouraging. I worked with Jerry Lewis after the *Colgate Comedy Hour* was over and he was doing his specials. I was going to run into Jerry Lewis years later. At that time, *Matinee Theater* was the "in" thing and live drama had the top stars at noon, which allowed many actors to go to work, but I never worked any of those shows. I observed on stage the great show that will never be forgotten — Mary Martin doing *Peter Pan*. I was able to meet Winston Churchill's daughter Sarah, who came out for *Matinee Theater*. I never got to work for *Matinee Theater* but I was allowed to sit in on the readings and the stagings of the show.

There were some sincere people at NBC who were in my corner and we are still very close friends. Tom Sarnoff, the son of General Sarnoff, who founded NBC, and I became great friends, and many people in the upper echelon at NBC knew the situation I was in but they could do nothing about it, because that was the social climate of the time. This was before the civil rights era, and NBC was trying to bring about some sort of equality within television broadcasting.

Just then, live TV was displaced by tape, and the fact is, not only was I dismissed from the stage, but a number of stage managers were dismissed at the same time. I thought, "Well, I got it made now, I can go to any TV company and get me a job!" Well, they weren't hiring any blacks. NBC found this out and asked me if I would come back to supervise the parking lot and also help set up for the new studios opening in Burbank. I had taken a year to see what was going on out in the world and I found out that every door was shut. So I went back to NBC. Back to the parking lot.

THE GREATEST STORY EVER TOLD

In the meantime I had become a member of the Radio and Television Directors Guild. In 1960 they joined hands with the Screen Directors Guild and became one union — the Directors Guild of America. So that automatically put this little boy in the Directors Guild. The only black member by a merger of two unions; that's how I got there. So I went to the stage managers' meetings and I was like a wart on a pole, I was just there. I was not part of anything, being that I was the only tadpole sitting on a lily pad.

I didn't push anymore because I felt defeated. Now, it's Directors Guild policy for members to seek out other members when hiring for a position. George Stevens was directing *The Greatest Story Ever Told*. It was the time of the civil rights movement, and George Stevens, being on the board of the Guild, had questioned whether there was a black person in the Guild. There was only one on the West Coast — Fred Lights being in New York — and that was me. I've been divided by the issue of tokenism, but I truly believe that there was more to it with this man. I think that in his heart it wasn't tokenism and he was really sincere in promoting a black man in filmmaking. At the same time, I think he knew that hiring a black man in this position was going to make news, and it did. The *New York Times, Newsweek* and every black newspaper in in the country, radio news, television news, covered the fact that I had been chosen as an assistant director. This was much to the chagrin of many members of the Guild who were assistant directors, who never had this kind of publicity before. Whites had never had this kind of publicity. Overnight, this brother became a news item. When I came back from location all the black members of the press were at the L.A. Airport. While none of the stars of the film were getting photographed, I was getting photographed. I was carried in *The New York Times*, and the daily press. George Stevens and *The Greatest Story Ever Told* gave me momentum. I was an instant celebrity, invited into circles I hereto had only read about. I say to everybody that you must have a father in this business. If you don't believe me, ask all the people who have succeeded in this business. Their fathers were somebody, or their mothers. In this way, I call George Stevens my father. I guess I have a white father in my life also.

So, I was in the NBC booth directing people where to park their cars, when the phone rang and they said "This is George Stevens Productions calling to speak to Wendell Franklin." I thought they were calling to see if they had a parking clearance for the day. The executive assistant director, Ray Gosnell, said, "Wendell Franklin, are you available for work?" I began to perspire and I said, "Yes" and he said, "Report out to Culver City at the old Selznick Studios to George Stevens Productions." I was paralyzed. I thought this couldn't happen. Somebody was kidding me. I had to call upstairs to personnel to see if I could be excused. So they said yes, and I went out to see Mr. Stevens. I couldn't believe I was sitting in the office of this man, a great director and a past president of the Guild.

All he said was, "Well, are you ready to go to work?" Francisco "Chico" Day, who was on the picture as one of the first assistants, began to get all his scripts and story breakdowns together for me. I ended up having about ten different books of how this show was to operate. It must have been a sight to see me lug these things back to the parking lot. In the meantime I had called back NBC and asked could I get my closeout check.

The whole studio knew about it and there were congratulations up and down the hall. They had gone out and bought me a briefcase, and inside the briefcase was $500 in cash. But please believe me, I had to leave the next day. A phone call at ten o'clock one morning, and leaving the next day at seven in the morning by private plane to Utah. So I had to run down to the Army and Navy store and get me a foot locker and some boots and some outdoor wear for up in the mountains. I had to carry this huge luggage of scripts, it looked like a Bible in itself: the breakdowns, the casting sheets for the stars.

I had a very beautiful apartment, but I just walked out and left it. I told others to put my stuff in storage, as I had no time to do it myself. Forget all the material I have around me, I'm gone. People said, "Well, you ought to let them wait a day or so." I said "You speak for yourself, I am gone. When opportunity knocks, you forget everything — the car, the clothes, the furniture, the grand piano and whatever, that's it!"

I've followed this philosophy all of my life: when opportunities present themselves, then you have to jump at them. So many people have turned away opportunity because they had to do this, that and the other. So there I was, leaving on this private plane, and about 20 people went to the airport to see me off. On the plane, I was called over by the head of the assistant directors. He asked me to sign a note that stated when I returned off of *The Greatest Story Ever Told* I would forget about being an assistant director and that I would return to television. I didn't care; I was ready to sign the Magna Carta or the Constitution at this particular time, I just wanted to get to work. Here was the one opportunity that had never been presented to a black man in this industry. So I signed the paper.

They sent down a chauffeur-driven car, a station wagon, to pick me up. There was an encampment of tents and cabins to accommodate 700 people, including all the stars. At that time Hollywood was in a good financial shape and Stevens was able to get the very best technical people from all over the studios. Here was a man who was an Academy Award winner for his pictures and who was able to hire two Academy Award-winning cinematographers.

When I got to the camp I thought I was the King of the Tournament of Roses, or something. There were all these people watching this little black boy with this big bear hat and leather jacket on as if to say, "Well, there he is." Suddenly I felt very lonesome. It took five days for them to finally settle where I was going to sleep. The other assistant directors lived on the front row street, but I ended up in the cabin behind them with the script supervisor.

On the set, I felt inadequate — I didn't know what a call sheet was or a breakdown, let alone filling out these forms. I was thrown into a whirlpool of many things that I thought were going to drown me. Nothing in my short career in television prepared me for motion picture work.

In stage management you do not get to be too personal with the director, he's up in the booth. All the people running the show are up in the booth and you're on the floor taking orders. At rehearsals, or at the reading of a show you sit at a table, you are not directly involved in the placement of things — what sets are to move out, what's to move in. You have a rundown of what's happening next, but television is so much different from film, especially live TV, because the booth runs the show and the stage manager never gets in the booth. You became more aware of people, the audience behind you, a thousand eyes looking over your shoulder. I knew the actor depended on me for his cue from the booth, because you had nothing else but cue cards then; there were no teleprompters. The director would tell the head stagehand when to fly this prop in, when to fly it back out, or give the signal to that particular stagehand. It's just a little difficult saying what you could bring from live TV to film, but I didn't see any comparisons whatsoever.

As fate would have it, things began to slowly come to me, I learned from this man's relationship with actors, and his sincerity of developing a role with an actor that was only three or four lines. Stevens the man was interested in me and Stevens the director was interested in everything that went on in his set. Here I learned you don't rush, you take your time and prepare.

Here was José Ferrer, Telly Savalas, Angela Lansbury, Charlton Heston, Max Von Sydow, Robert Blake, David Hedison, Van Heflin, Sal Mineo. Perhaps the greatest cast and greatest crew ever assembled worked this film. At night when I dropped the call sheets off at their bungalows, it might be snowing up to my boots, but they offered cordiality, warmth and support. They were aware of my shortcomings, but on that set, Stevens never let on that he knew about it. He treated me as if I had been an assistant director for the last twenty years.

So *The Greatest Story Ever Told* to me has the greatest impact on my life as far as film is concerned. Here was my learning tree, my experience to learn something. But it was done the hard way. Nobody wanted to show me anything. Everybody in the production office was trying to get rid of me, but Stevens was not going to have it. I was and am black, but here was a man who would not allow any shortcomings on location or whatever, and there were many incidents of prejudice that I have to consider during this period. Hollywood crews had never had any black ADs around telling them what to do and how to do it, where to walk, and how to move. It was an experience for them also. There were many who resented me. Most of these men had been hard, encrusted filmmakers for twenty-five years ahead of me and they had never imagined blacks would be involved behind the scenes. They had lived in their own world which was a racist world, and there's no sense denying that now. John Veitch and Ray Gosnell, the first assistant directors, were the only other crew members who showed any good feelings towards me. John later became a vice-president at Columbia. Stevens staffed all of his departments with assistant directors on this picture. Transportation or whatever, they were all headed by assistant directors. But we were also on the stage. There were three firsts and four seconds and I was one of the seconds. Three firsts!

I was carried away by the talents of the assistant directors who were famous in this business for staging colossal productions like *Ben Hur*. Anybody brought into the atmosphere I was exposed to would also have been in awe. The grandness of big sets and mountains that were hewed out to make sets!

I'll always remember the morning that we opened the beginning of the picture. It was the River Galilee sequence when a rabbi, a Protestant minister, and a Catholic priest poured their different types of holy waters into the waters of the Colorado River.

This was spectacle! There were four thousand extras, people of the community of Utah. We were shooting in the mountains for almost six months. Not only in Utah, but Nevada and many of the mountainous regions in that area, which looked more like the Holy Land than the real Holy Land looked because that had been modernized with hotels. Now all those huge colossal sets are under water.

I'll never forget the majesty of Max Von Sydow coming down in those robes on that set. If ever there has been an image of Jesus that has been realistic to me, this was it and we were reverent; no cursing was allowed on the sets. We had almost four thousand people on the set, of all races. This was the first biblical picture with black people. There were black people at this time because Africans were in the Holy Land. Stevens was an honest man; he had the foresight to do it right. When we returned to Los Angeles to shoot, there were black nuns and dancers at the court of Herod, women and men were all included in this, it was fantastic. When Christ chased the money-changers from the tables, Stevens had black men sitting there. There were black Jews, black Hebrews, Yemenites, there were many people of history who were a dark color.

When we shot the Via Dolorosa sequence, which is now known as the Stations of the Cross, it was just fantastic. When Jesus was on his way to Calgary, Simon — Sidney Poitier — picked up the cross, and that was one of the greatest moments in my life, for it was the first time that the truth was told. The Bible even depicts that it was a black man who picks up the cross, but we had never seen that in motion pictures before. There has never been a biblical picture made that used so many people of color. That's why I honor the Stevens picture, because people of my race were used throughout, in every essence, even down to soldiers. I think that Stevens using blacks and other people of color on this picture was making a statement. This is a religious picture which is played every Easter and Christmas throughout the world.

Another memorable scene was the Resurrection, when the healed blind man struggles to the gates. The crucifixion was shot on the stage — the three crosses being raised with Max in the middle of the two thieves, and Ed Wynn coming to the gate as the former blind man wanting to see this man, because Jesus had restored his sight. Down below on the lower edge of the stage was Joseph Schildkraut as Nicodemus and Dorothy Maguire as Mary the mother. David Hedison gave those great lines when he turned to Mary: "Mother, see thy son. Son, see thy mother." As the crucifixes began to be raised by the soldiers pulling huge ropes, with thunder and lightning everywhere, even the crew went into tears. It was one of the most dramatic moments I have ever seen on the stage. There was this great ethereal music, with Stevens at the dials turning it up and the choir all on the set at the same time; it was a mind blower. This film was my birth into filmmaking.

Several little problems came up for me. I used to go to the Yemenites' services on Fridays and wear my yarmulke. A gentleman who was on the executive staff of Mr. Stevens' company, a former executive of MGM, told me that I should go to my cabin at six o'clock in the evening and forget about going to services. Well, Stevens stopped that. He berated that particular gentleman enough for him to get so upset that he resigned from the picture. At this time there was civil rights, there was burning of cities in Chicago and Los Angeles and Detroit and there was a similar kind of feeling brewing in Hollywood. Nevertheless, due to the fact that the doors to behind the camera in Hollywood had been closed to blacks all the time, my presence was a kind of a threat. The civil rights movement was moving into their backyard.

On returning to L.A., George Stevens premiered *The Greatest Story Ever Told* at the Cinerama Dome in Hollywood, every night for seven nights. To illustrate what a great man Stevens was, one of the premieres was in honor of Dr. Martin Luther King. It was a sold out performance, with the money going for the Freedom March. Marlon Brando and Robert Wise, and many people who I was to know later in my life were all a part of the Martin Luther King team. Stevens was right there in the thick of it. I'll never forget Stevens, Brando, and Dr. King entering the theater together that night.

My church sponsored the Sunday night screening, and I feel very fortunate in that I was the only assistant director, I believe, to ever be honored with a premiere. It was a sold out house, with red carpet service. All for a second assistant director's premiere — hello! That night, Dan Duryea presented me with a plaque from Los Angeles

City Council and I received another plaque — the Churchmen's Award. That was a memorable night in my life. Previously, my church had had the pleasure of sending for Martin Luther King to come to Los Angeles for the first time. I had the pleasure of presenting him on my roster for Men's Day. That afternoon I had the honor of going to the microphone at the Sports Arena and presenting him along with Mahalia Jackson and a thousand-voice choir. There were seventeen thousand people inside the arena and twenty thousand outside. That's the way Martin Luther King was first received in Los Angeles.

When Martin Luther King was assassinated, I was at Warner Bros. at the time and the set just stood still. I mean all the sets on the lot. After we went back to work, Eli Landau came on the lot and said they were going to do this tribute to Martin Luther King on film. The tribute would appear in five thousand theaters for one night at five dollars per person, and the funds would be used to establish a Martin Luther King Foundation. Bill Cosby offered his entire staff and crew to do the show. I was first assistant then and so this was a pleasure. Clarence Williams of *The Mod Squad*, Charlton Heston, Sammy Davis, Jr., Ben Gazzara, you name them — some of the biggest stars in Hollywood came out. It was put together by Eli Landau in less than twenty-four hours. There was some of the most beautiful poetry in the world. This was just for this one night and I've never seen it again. Nobody has. But it sold out across America in five thousand theaters and each theater seated two to three thousand. This happened very shortly after his burial.

UNIVERSAL STUDIOS

After my employment with *The Greatest Story Ever Told* ended, I went to Stevens and told him that the Guild wouldn't let me move over to the film side of the business. Stevens called me from Washington and said don't worry about it. Next thing I know, the Guild had a meeting about whether to vote me in. They were very argumentative at the Assistant Directors Council and the assistant directors had to vote me in as a full assistant director. There was a lot of confrontation, and it was finally put to a vote. I was present at the meeting, which is why I remember it so well.

In the meantime, they had voted in about forty other new assistant directors. At that time the studios put up one person a year, as did the director members of the Guild. Hollywood has always been a closed door, I don't care how open they think it is. Nepotism was reigning then and it reigns now. I might be criticized for saying this, but it's true. That's why I call George Stevens my father in the business. At least in the symbolic sense, I had a father to stand up for me. In the meeting, somebody finally jumped up and talked about the civil rights movement and how the Guild could cause itself some problems by not allowing admission to blacks. The Guild has always been for integration in the arts as far as I'm concerned; it's been the leader in trying to bring about affirmative action in the Hollywood area. Anyway, because of the issue of possible bad publicity, I was allowed to enter into the Guild in 1962 as a second assistant director. But it was about six or seven months before I had a job.

I wasn't getting work, so I called George Stevens and he called Jim Pratt, head of production over at Universal. After a while Jim called me and that's when I went to work for Universal, which lasted that first time for five years. My first picture for Universal was *McHale's Navy* with Ernest Borgnine and Tim Conway.

Of the many, many feature pictures that I had a chance to be involved with at Universal there are some people who do stand out. First there is Jim Pratt, Shirley MacLaine, Tony Randall, Leslie Caron, Gina Lollobrigida, Victor Buono, Rock Hudson, Lana Turner, Dan Duryea and his son especially. These people accepted me as more than an assistant director. During the civil rights period, some people were very surprised when I would come on their sets, but these people were very good to me. This even caused a little controversy when others thought that I should stay in my place. My support came chiefly from the actors.

Some of my directors gave me a hard time, and I even remember when I did a call sheet or a production report and the production office would make a point of double checking to see if I had the comma in the right place. They would usually find something wrong. When I first came to Universal, on my first day, a unit manager for *McHale's Navy* said to me, "Remember you're representing your people, and remember what you do here is so very important." I resented that. I wasn't representing my people, I was representing Wendell Franklin, even though whatever I did was for the betterment of other blacks being hired.

My story is different because I don't think that any Caucasian assistant director experienced the insensitivity that I went through, being made to feel inferior. Being a very strong and aggressive person, I just said "Well to hell with it!" and I meant it. I remember when I walked into Universal, several of those old stage hands who had been around for eighty years, didn't appreciate me being there and said aloud, "Oh, we got a nigger on the set." In 1965, if a man on a show was 60 years old, you knew he was a prejudiced man, I don't care how you looked at it, period. In the rest rooms at Universal, there would be nasty racial epithets on the walls, and I think they had to scrub and repaint them several times.

Which is interesting, because Universal was my grounding, my education in film. After a few pictures, I was put on staff. It isn't like it is now, when you finish a picture you've got to go look for another job. I stayed at Universal. I saw the black towers go up, the tours become part of Universal Studios and all the expansion.

I remember meeting Ann-Margret on her first picture — *Kitten With a Whip* — which was my second feature at Universal. The picture was just a little too naughty, so I don't think too many people ever saw it. I recently saw her doing *The Two Mrs. Grenvilles* and I thought about how she has become such a fabulous star. I was talking to my good friend George Sidney, director of *Bye, Bye, Birdie,* and we agreed that at last, she has bloomed as a major actress.

I worked as a daily assistant on features like *Madame X, How to Save a Marriage (And Ruin Your Life),* and *Gaily,*

Gaily. When you were on studio payroll, as I was at Universal, you would replace someone as they sat down to eat, or if there was a scene with a lot of extras and you were needed to help. Those were the grand old days of motion pictures. They stopped keeping the production crews on staff in the late sixties, I think, for economic reasons. Economy is everything in this business.

Most of my work at Universal was features. I was a second assistant on one television show, *Farraday and Son*, starring Dan Dailey. I had worked with Rock Hudson on a couple of features, so he requested me for his television show, *McMillan and Wife*. He was truly a gentleman. I had the fortune of going to his house for the wrap of the show. My girlfriend and I went to his home, and we met his housekeeper who was black. We sat around the fireplace all night long with the dogs, then wound up staying for breakfast. Stella Stevens was a very beautiful and outgoing person I shall never forget. I think I've had the opportunity to know many personalities much closer than the average assistant director. I went to their homes, much to the consternation of the studio heads. I think it's standard practice — not based on race, but on the hierarchy of the set — that the assistant director does not become a part of the social life of the top stars of their studio.

I particularly remember my daily work on *The Night Walker*, directed by William Castle. We were shooting at night over on Wilshire Boulevard by the Masonic Temple, and the streets had all been cleared. Right across the street is a famed house that had been used for mystery pictures, so we wanted to do a travelling shot turning up Crenshaw to Wilshire Boulevard and turning right where the Masonic Temple was. They had me stationed on the corner behind the slat, to notify the set when the camera crew and the principal were driving and making the left hand turn into the mansion. It's night, it's dark and Wilshire Boulevard is almost vacant. I'm standing with my walkie-talkie right on Wilshire Boulevard and the police drive up and grab me, slam me upside the wall. At that point, Terrence Nelson, the first assistant director, got out of the camera car and said "Hey, this is a motion picture." The only thing I remember saying on my walkie-talkie was "Light the goddamn set now!" All the LAPD could see was this black man standing on the corner of Wilshire Boulevard with a big leather jacket on. And then every light went up. The policeman said he didn't know if I was trying to deliver dope or what.

FUNNY GIRL

After leaving Universal, I went to Twentieth Century Fox. I worked on *The Monroes,* Barbara Hershey's first TV series. Remember, I had worked on nothing but features at Universal for a number of years. At Twentieth, I worked on two or three TV series: *Tammy Grimes, The Green Hornet.* Then things faded out like they always do, studios' fortunes go up and down, so I went to Columbia. When I walked into Columbia I felt like I was a very well qualified man as an assistant director, but Columbia too was a great, great learning experience. I had the chance to work on *Who's Minding the Mint?* with Victor Buono, Dorothy Provine, and Milton Berle. I worked on *How to Save a Marriage (And Ruin Your Life)* with Eli Wallach and Dean Martin, Anne Jackson. Walter Brennan was a beautiful person. *Enter Laughing* was Carl Reiner's debut as a motion picture director. Here I had the chance to work with the fabulous Elaine May and Shelley Winters, and José Ferrer.

Model Shop, with Jacques Demy directing, was a wonderful experience in filmmaking. He was French and could hardly speak English. We shot right in the middle of West Hollywood, we stopped traffic in the center of the street at Beverly and Fairfax. At 5 o'clock in the afternoon we had traffic tied up across town four different ways, much to the chagrin of the Los Angeles Police Department. All of the film was shot here in Los Angeles. We used actual massage parlors and pool halls. We filmed on Santa Monica Boulevard and in all the streets with travelling cameras. As second assistant, this was a chance for me to see a director from another country who felt no pain in achieving what he wanted. Whatever he wanted he was going to get for that camera come hell or high water. Gary Lockwood, who would later be the star of *2001: A Space Odyssey*, was great to work with. This was a momentous picture in teaching me about direction; the principles of feeling, atmosphere, utilizing actual environments where there were real live sets of stores with people in them. By watching Demy direct, I learned how to capitalize on the nature of real life and to take what would seem like a bad or confusing camera setup, and to turn it around so that it worked for the film.

Another picture at Columbia was *Three on a Couch* with Jerry Lewis starring and directing. San Francisco was a most marvelous location, and Jerry decided to take the whole company out on the town the night before we began to shoot. We all were staying at the Mark Hopkins and Jerry had me call the club to find out who was playing — it was Ramsey Lewis. Jerry had me reserve the club and we all went out that evening. Jerry rode on the cable cars while they threw me in the limousine and the whole cast and crew went. We partied, and Jerry even played the drums. We had an eight o'clock shoot the next morning, but none of us made it to the docks on time. We had rented this great big ocean liner "The Roosevelt," which was waiting for us. We finally arrived on the docks to shoot at ten o'clock, but we had to rent about a hundred taxi cabs to all get there in time. What a night and what a day that was! Working with Jerry Lewis was more like going to an event every day.

Columbia was a great experience for me because John Veitch was executive producer and Howard Pine was unit manager on the films. The best time was on *Funny Girl*. Herb Ross was the choreographer and William Wyler was the director. Here was this outgoing woman — a Broadway actress with an attitude, who would surely not be accepted on the Hollywood scene — named Barbra Streisand. She had problems, but she persevered and even won the Academy Award with her first picture. My work with Streisand was wonderful. She cared. She was a champion of civil rights, too. Shooting right next door was *Guess Who's Coming to Dinner?* with Sidney Poitier, Spencer Tracy, and Katharine Hepburn. Hepburn and Streisand would share the Academy Award for that year [the Best Actress Oscar for 1968 was shared by Streisand for *Funny Girl* and Hepburn for *The Lion in Winter*. Hepburn had won the Best Actress Oscar for 1967 for *Guess Who's Coming to Dinner?* Ed.]. The lot was alive, it was electric!

The first three or four months on *Funny Girl* we spent rehearsing. At lunchtime on the set I had a habit of saying, "Anybody need hamburgers, I'm going down to the commissary, and I'll be glad to bring them back?" Well, one day I was going to meet somebody for lunch. Everybody ran up to me to get their hamburgers as usual, and I had to tell them that I wasn't getting them today. This one particular gentleman said, "What do you mean, you're not going to get them today? Get them or you'll be fired!" So I said "Well, I'll tell you one thing, my contract with the Directors Guild working here at Columbia does not make me a waiter. You'll have to get your own lunch today." This was still during rehearsals. He called the front office and caused a hullabaloo, but he found out that the Directors Guild did not want me to be a waiter.

During *Funny Girl,* Streisand was getting ready for her first big concert at the Hollywood Bowl. She'd given everybody tickets in the reserved section. She gave me four tickets in a reserved box in the garden section of the Hollywood Bowl. Not thinking, I left my tickets on the assistant directors' desk on the stage. It seems that certain members of the dance company found out where my tickets were located, two levels ahead of them at the Bowl. I don't think Barbra was thinking about discrimination when she gave me the box seats. She just said "Well, I think I'll just put Wendell here and that's all..." A big fuss started over that, and Barbra, bless her heart, changed all of their seats. Streisand to me will always be a great lady, because she let this incident run off of her like water off a duck's back.

Funny Girl was an unusual experience. I'm one of the few, if not the only, black assistant directors that have worked a feature musical. A musical is altogether different than anything else in feature pictures. You have to learn how the cuts are made, how you shoot with extras in a theater to make the theater appear full. I never could have learned this in a school. I got news for you. I could hardly assist, I could hardly direct, because my mouth was still wide open about the sets, the gowns, the lighting, the orchestra and the choreography. I was a little Los Angeles yokel boy and the only time I'd seen these big musicals is when they were on the screen, but here I was actually on this production. I would just get lost standing in the middle of the stage. Somebody had to call my name twice to get my attention, because I was so in awe.

I'll never forget the night that Streisand sang "People (Who Need People)" on the Columbia Ranch, at three in the morning. Herb Ross took the crane and top shot it. She was at a lamp post, and when she began to sing, I couldn't help it, the tears came. It was the emotion of "this was motion pictures, this was feature pictures" that got me. When that crane came down and she began to walk back to the store on the corner, baby I was shook. I went home and I couldn't sleep. I'm an emotional person and I laugh when something is funny, and I cry when something is tearful. I remember working as a daily on *Madame X*. In Lana Turner's death scene, her son comes into the jail, but he doesn't know that she's his mother. I got news for you, everybody else was hard-bitten on that crew, but I sat up there and just drizzled tears. I hope I never lose sight of the emotional factor. It's not kosher, you know, to have any feelings on a set. The whole time I've been in this business, I've always lived every emotion that happens in a picture. I have seen some actors and actresses that have brought a director so much impact on a set.

Barbra and I developed a rapport, as I was the one to bring her onto the set each day. She was married to Elliott Gould at that time, and there was a new baby. Her wardrobe mistress was a black woman who had not yet gotten into the union. So this woman would dress Barbra in the trailer and then when she came out, the union wardrobe person would take over. I'd be the one to go to the trailer and say "Miss Streisand, we're ready." She'd say, "Come on in, Wendell, I'm still getting ready." The film crew wanted to know why she wasn't there on the set right away. She was, I have to admit, late many times. Being the second assistant director on the picture, the producers of *Funny Girl* came down to push me to sign a paper saying that I witnessed the fact that Barbra Streisand had run up sixty or seventy thousand dollars on the budget due to her lateness. I told them I wasn't going to sign anything, the production report would show it. The production report is the law, god and bible of a motion picture. You could go back twenty years on a lawsuit with that production report, because everything is recorded there. After you make it out on that stage, it goes from the production office to every area of money or executive responsibility in the studio. They all read it. When they read this particular one, they all fell out with me. But Columbia stood behind me, and finally Howard Pine and Johnny Veitch said you don't have to sign anything but the production report. The producer of the picture has disliked me ever since.

MEDIUM COOL

Columbia cooled down for a while and I was walking across the Paramount lot when somebody said, "You want a picture?" That was my chance for *Medium Cool*, to be directed by Haskell Wexler, who I did not know at the time. I did know he was one of the industry's greatest cameramen. This was to be his first directing experience.

So, into Chicago we went, and we stayed at the big fabulous Sherman Hotel which was owned by the Wexler family. We had two or three floors and the garage, keeping all of our equipment there. The Wexlers are almost an institution in Chicago. Just about nine-tenths of everything in Chicago was Wexler, they are a very distinguished family.

This particular picture took me from second assistant director to first. I don't think we were in Chicago two weeks and preparing to shoot when the first assistant, Erich von Stroheim, Jr., took ill and had to go to the hospital. He was then transported back to Hollywood, where he died. I was automatically moved up to first assistant with the approval of the Directors Guild. I had prayed that it would happen someday, but unfortunately it had to come about through a circumstance like this. Then the unit manager decided to leave because Chicago was hot. The Democratic Convention was hot. Mayor Daley had already had our rooms searched, looking for scripts to try and find out what we were going to shoot in Chicago. And so I became unit manager also.

As I said before, Mayor Daley and his cronies were worried about our script. Haskell wouldn't let anyone have the script; even Paramount hadn't seen it. The police department searched our rooms night and day, looking for scripts. All the scripts had been purposefully destroyed. It was just amazing how Haskell shot it out of his head.

Now, on the convention floor, the galleries were all white, but Mayor Daley saw how the vote was going. So he commanded all the black employees of Chicago under his reign to attend the convention when it was time for the big vote. You looked up in the balcony the next day, it was solid black, Mayor Daley said you either be here or you're fired. That meant all the garbage people, all the service people, all the city workers — Mayor Daley ran Chicago, he owned Chicago.

We caught Mayor Daley's famous vulgar epithet on camera, which to me if you see it in *Medium Cool* is one of the most remarkable pieces of candid drama that was never planned.

It was my first experience with reality and documentary technique in a motion picture. Haskell would get the real thing; if we needed winos we would go in the street and get winos. For the early morning disco scene, we put flyers out the night before and got seven hundred to a thousand kids at this disco at seven o'clock in the morning. Haskell's taste was for a reality almost too real; drama with a documentary influence. For example, in order to shoot the fatal accident which closes the picture, we tied up the expressways beginning at four o'clock in the morning.

When Haskell shot in the basement of the hotel, he wanted to do a scene where the winos would come into the first aid station to be blood tested. So we created that station. The production assistants went and got real winos and we had gallons of wine for them. Now if there is anything that is interpreted by this film, it's the reality; these were not actors, these were people who were the real thing. When we had the big press party in the picture all the members of the press in Chicago were invited and there was a cocktail party at nine o'clock in the morning. We had the booze out, and if you see the picture, you can watch them getting stoned; all this was real.

At the London House, which was one of the most prestigious clubs of Chicago, Dorothy Donnagat was appearing. I knew Dorothy very well, because she had appeared in many of the benefit shows I had done in Los Angeles in previous years. We're all sitting here in the nightclub having dinner, and we hear this noise popping in the streets—that was the beginning of the riots. I believe the next day was a Sunday, and Haskell phoned me and said, "I don't need the full crew today." So Haskell, myself, and the sound team went out to the park which was right by the Arena.

Here was mass confusion, the police were beating people in the head with billy sticks. But Haskell with that camera ran through all this and if you've seen *Medium Cool* you'll see some of the most memorable live scenes that have ever been put on film of an actual riot. The crew got sprayed with mace. Mace was sprayed by the police on everyone. I don't want to make an incident out of it. Like I got maced, but thousands of people got maced. People went to the hospital on account of having billy clubs upside their head. A policeman struck down on our sound man's head. I'll never forget this, they had tanks, barbed wires, the National Guard, it looked like warfare. I consider Haskell one of the most daring men to go into an environment like this to capture one of the most famous and infamous conventions that has ever been held.

We shot in the convention hall and, believe it or not, at first we couldn't get entrance to the convention. So I told Haskell, I think I know a way. I said I want to put a call in to Washington, to George Stevens, Jr., because he and Pierre Salinger were close. I put a call in to 1900 Pennsylvania Avenue, everybody stood up in the office and said are you kidding, you're calling the White House? I called and got hold of George Stevens, Jr. and he turned me over to Pierre Salinger. I first told Stevens, Jr. that this was Wendell Franklin, I had been the assistant director on his father's picture and he had told me that anything you wanted to go with the picture, you go to the source. I said to Stevens, Jr. — now you're the source. We are shooting here in Chicago and we want to get into the convention. So he got Salinger for me, and I've never met Pierre Salinger, but in less than twenty-four hours, he had gotten us complete clearance above newspeople and everyone else to go into the Chicago Convention Center and shoot. I felt very, very proud of myself. We went the day before the convention was to open and got our cameras in place, and put our two principals into seating where we were going to shoot them attending the convention. So this was about as real as it gets.

Other scenes were more staged. The last scene, when the car crashes, was dramatized, but Haskell was a director who could afford to do his own film how he wanted to. He's a good creative man; he can create without a piece of paper. He had the position to do it. He didn't have a big producer sitting over his back. He didn't have Paramount watching his every move; I don't think he even let Paramount see any of the footage, until it was edited. At the end of the film, he's up on this scaffold with his camera. I think that was a pure impulse of what he felt at that time. That's the reason why I consider him an unusual, almost avant garde director.

The footage of the black family, when the guy finds the money, was planned. That was a dramatization with actors. Felton Perry, who plays the taxi cab driver, came to Hollywood and did wonderful things like *Brian's Song*; he was from Evanston, Illinois. The people who played the Blackstone Rangers on screen, who wanted him to share the money, they were members of the actual Blackstone Rangers, but they were also actors. We shot on the north side of Chicago, up in the black, Italian, and Jewish area. The scenes were for real, but they were all professional actors.

We had to pay to shoot in a black neighborhood, like you pay in any neighborhood. You can shoot anywhere you want, you can shoot in West Hell if you got the money. But on the north side of Chicago, there was this family with a little boy. When we first moved up to this area, the buildings were in such bad shape that they all leaned to the right. They were about to fall over and I mean they leaned. We had the family and all the people who lived in this three story building all move out, and the crew moved in. Haskell put this little boy, who never knew anything about motion pictures, at the center of attention of *Medium Cool.*

Wendell Franklin on the parking lot at NBC with Dinah Shore, 1950.

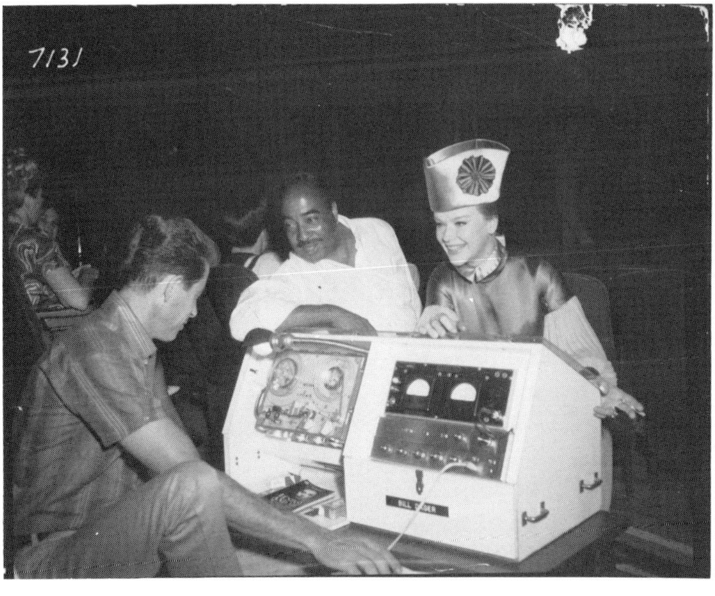

TV in the 1950s: Wendell Franklin (center) with Anne Francis.

Wendell Franklin and an unidentified actress from *Living Between Two Worlds* (1963), a film written and produced by Horace Jackson. Wendell Franklin helped to promote the film, and arranged a prestigious screening at the Directors Guild Theater in Hollywood.

Living Between Two Worlds — **(left to right) singer Skip Trineir, the film's director Bobby Johnson, (unidentified), Wendell Franklin.**

Living Between Two Worlds — **(from left) Reverend A.E. Williams, Sal Mineo, Horace Jackson, (unidentified), Wendell Franklin.** *Photo by Cliff Hall.*

The Directors Guild of America screening party for *Living Between Two Worlds* — (left to right, standing) Horace Jackson, U.S. Congressman Mervyn M. Dymally, Charlton Heston, Wendell Franklin, Laszlo Kovacs (the film's cinematographer, with Vilmos Zsigmond), Lily Mae Austin, Mimi Dillard (lead actress in the film), and [first name unknown] Johnson; (from left, kneeling) Kyle Johnson (actor in the film), DeForest Covan.

Living Between Two Worlds' DGA screening — (left to right, standing) (unidentified), Laszlo Kovacs, Wendell Franklin, writer-producer Frank Gardonyi, Mimi Dillard, Vilmos Zsigmond, (unidentified woman), Mervyn Dymally, Woody Strode (center, back), (four unidentified), DeForest Covan, (unidentified, with champagne bottle); (left to right, bottom) Nappy Whiting, Horace Jackson, Lily Mae Austin.

Wendell Franklin (center, checkered sweater) on location for *The Greatest Story Ever Told* **(1965).**

Assistant Director Wendell Franklin on the set of *The Greatest Story Ever Told*.

Wendell Franklin at the DGA, during the making of *The Greatest Story Ever Told*.

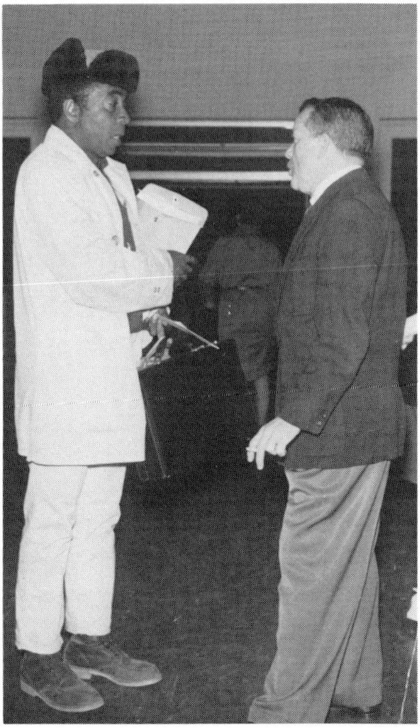

Wendell Franklin on the set of *The Favor* **(released as** *A Very Special Favor*, **Universal, 1965).**

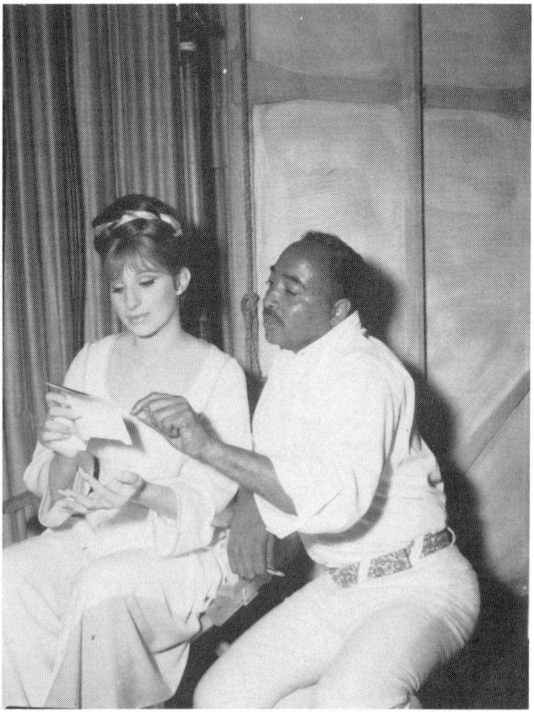

On the set of *Funny Girl*, **1967 — Barbra Streisand, Wendell Franklin.**

Wendell Franklin in his Hollywood apartment on Kings Road, 1960s-70s.

Wendell Franklin in the Kings Road apartment.

Wendell Franklin had friends drive him around the block on Sunset Boulevard, according to Horace Jackson, "literally 1,000 times" to view this billboard for *The Bus is Coming* **(1971).**

Wendell Franklin instructs young actors in *The Bus is Coming*. **In the background: producer Horace Jackson.** *Photo from the Directors Guild of America* **Action** *Magazine, Jan.-Feb. 1972*

Red carpet is rolled out in Compton (Los Angeles) for director Wendell Franklin at the premiere of his film, *The Bus is Coming* in 1971.

As part of the Directors Guild of America's 50th anniversary celebration in 1986, pioneering black director Oscar Micheaux was recognized for his film achievements with a star on Hollywood's Walk of Fame. From left (kneeling in foreground): Johnny Grant, William Crain, Micheaux' niece Verna Crowe (holding plaque), Wendell Franklin, (unidentified), Bill Welsh (Hollywood Chamber of Commerce). Also present: (from left, standing) Ted Lange, Raymond St. Jacques (in fringed jacket), DGA president Gilbert Cates (left of podium), Robert Wise (center, at microphone), George Sidney (standing, right of podium), Luther James (next right, in hat), and Roger E. Mosley (far back, left of tree). *Photo: David Shepard, Jr.; from the* Directors Guild of America Newsletter *March 1987.*

DGA Oscar Micheaux tribute, 1986 — (from left) William Crain, Micheaux' niece Verna Crowe, Wendell Franklin, Sidney Poitier. *Photos by Howard Morehead.*

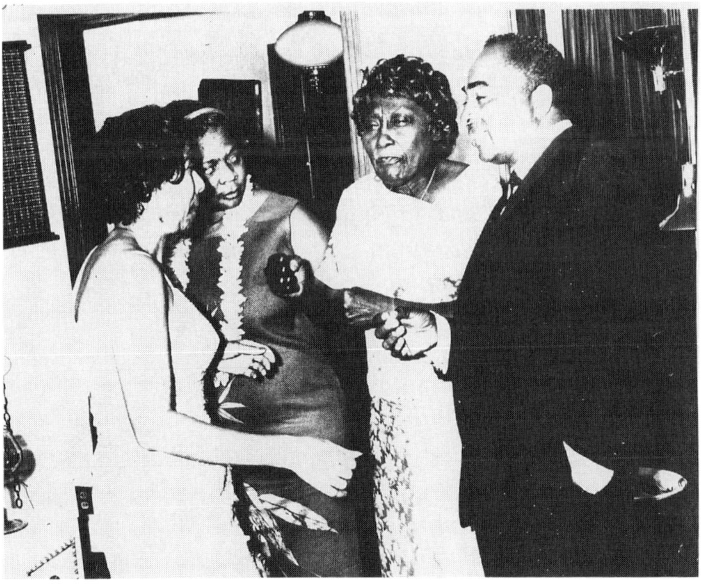

Wendell Franklin with actress A.C. Harris Bilbrew, who appeared in the first black all-talking motion picture, *Hearts in Dixie* **(1929).**

T•
IPM90CA
1-0018671I137 05/17/86
TLX WU TFC A LSA DLY PD
ZCZC 003 DLY 05-17 831A PDT
PMS DLR
HOLLYWOOD CA
BT
LDA026(1008)(1-001821I137002)PD 05/17/86 1002
TWX WHITEHOUSE WSH DLY PD
242 GOVT DLY WHITE HOUSE DC MAY 17
PMS MR. GILBERT CATES, (DLR DONT DWR)
PRESIDENT
DIRECTORS GUILD OF AMERICA
7950 SUNSET BOULEVARD
LOS ANGELES, CALIFORNIA 90046

I AM DELIGHTED TO SEND GREETINGS TO EVERYONE AT THE SPECIAL PROGRAM HONORING THE MEMORY OF OSCAR MICHEAUX AND ESPECIALLY CONGRATULATIONS TO HIS FAMILY AS THEY RECEIVE THE POSTHUMOUS SPECIAL ACHIEVEMENT AWARD IN HIS NAME

OSCAR MICHEAUX STANDS TALL IN THE HISTORY OF THE CINEMA -- FOR THE OBSTACLES HE OVERCAME, AND FOR THE OBSTACLES NOBODY IN HIS DAY COULD OVERCOME. NOTHING DAUNTED HIM, AND HIS WORK REMAINS AS A TESTAMENT TO COURAGE AND ARTISTIC EXCELLENCE.

NANCY JOINS ME IN WISHING YOU A MEMORABLE PROGRAM AND CONTINUED SUCCESS. GOD BLESS YOU.

RONALD REAGAN
NNNN
1037 EST
•
IPM90CA

Telex from President Ronald Reagan for the Oscar Micheaux tribute.

```
◆
IPM90CA
1-013332I136002 05/16/86
TLX WUPUETLXALSA DLY PD
ZCZC 002 )6 DLY 05-16 140P PDT
PMS DLR
HOLLYWOOD CA
ET
 LDA101(1442)(1-012699A136)PD 05/16/86 1440
ICS IPMRYND RNO
05441 RENO NV 05-16 1237P PDT RYNC
ICS IPMLD04
4-026633S136 05/16/86
ICS IPMRNCZ CSP
  2134852121 TDRN LOS ANGELES CA 102 05-16 0214P EST
PMS WENDELL FRANKLIN
FILM DIRECTORS GUILD RPT DLY MGM, DLR ASAP, DLR
7950 SUNSET BLVD
HOLLYWOOD CA 90046

AS MAYOR OF THE CITY OF LOS ANGELES, ON EEHALF OF ITS CITIZENS, IT IS
A GREAT PLEASURE FOR ME TO EXTEND MY WARM AND SINCERE CONGRATULATIONS
TO OSCAR MICHEAUX, PIONEER ELACK FILM DIRECTOR, ON THE OCCASION OF
THE 50TH ANNIVERSARY CELEERATION OF THE FILM DIRECTORS GUILD, SUNDAY
MAY 18, 1986.

OSCAR MICHEAUX, THIS IS CERTAINLY A VERY SPECIAL TIME IN YOUR LIFE
AND I AM HONORED TO JOIN WITH OTHER LEADERS OF THE COMMUNITY IN
COMMENDING YOUR MANY OUTSTANDING CONTRIEUTIONS TO THE FILM INDUSTRY.
EEST WISHES FOR A MOST ENJOYAELE CELEERATION AND MAY THE FUTURE ERING
YOU CONTINUED SUCCESS.
SINCERELY,
  TOM ERADLEY
  MAYOR
  CITY OF LOS ANGELES
  200 NORTH SPRING ST
  LOS ANGELES CA 90012

1416 EST
 NNNN
1546 EST
◆
IPM90CA
```

Telex from Los Angeles Mayor Tom Bradley. Others who sent congratulatory telegrams and letters included George Sidney/DGA, Robert Wise/DGA, Gilbert Cates/DGA, The National Association of Media Women, and The Black Filmmakers Hall of Fame.

Some of those attending Wendell Franklin's funeral: William Crain (2nd from left), former Los Angeles Mayor Tom Bradley (4th from left), and (from right) the former Mrs. Wendell Franklin, Wendell Franklin's son Wendell Valentine, and Sidney Poitier.

Former Los Angeles Mayor Tom Bradley presents the U.S. flag to Wendell Franklin's godson, Adam-Brant Franklin Smith, during the funeral service.

County of Los Angeles Board of Supervisors

IN MEMORIAM

THE LOS ANGELES COUNTY BOARD OF SUPERVISORS
EXTENDS ITS DEEPEST SYMPATHY TO YOU
IN THE PASSING OF

YOUR BELOVED GRANDFATHER
WENDELL J. FRANKLIN

IN WHOSE MEMORY
ALL MEMBERS ADJOURNED IN TRIBUTE AND
REVERENCE AT ITS MEETING OF

JULY 26 1994

YVONNE BRATHWAITE BURKE
Chair of the Board
Supervisor, Second District

Wendell Franklin, 1987.

There was another little boy who I'll never forget, who came in through the alley on our "lean-to" set. There were rats in the alley where he was playing and some of them looked like lions, and this little white kid had marks where the rats had bit his feet. The wardrobe lady, the props man and I got this little boy and gave him a bath; he was so dirty and filthy. All of the crew chipped in to put some clothes on him. We found out he hadn't seen his mother and father in a whole week. He was just wandering up and down the alleys eating out of garbage cans. This had such an impact on me.

For drivers, we hired two members of the Blackstone Rangers and two of the Disciples, two of the most militant gangs in Chicago. They did not get along with each other. But we hired two of each for our four station wagons. Now up here in downtown Chicago everybody got along beautifully. So we moved out to 63rd and Cottage, which was near the gym where Mohammed Ali trained for years. We did the boxing scenes for *Medium Cool* there. I decided to lunch with these four guys who were driving. Down 63rd Street was a shop of African curiosities and I wanted to buy some carvings, so when I got ready to cross the street, the Blackstone Rangers stayed on this side of 63rd Street and the Disciples went across, and they said we don't cross each other's territory.

In the midst of all of this, there was a black woman, who was as big and round as two tables, I forget this woman's name but I'll call her "Big Mary." We shot at the welfare department, and the staff didn't know where the people's checks were, whether they were in the file or in the mail. She walked in and said, "Now, you bitches are going to come up with some checks this afternoon for these people or else I'm going to tear up this welfare office!" I want you to know that all those people — blacks, whites and Hispanics — got their checks that afternoon. That's on film. Haskell went right where the action was.

Haskell was a man who dared. The unions came down on us, because we didn't take the full crew out to shoot the riots, but there was no way to take that big crew. The man paid his crew, even if he didn't use them. Haskell had to be operating the camera — he's a man who can hold a camera straight at a million miles an hour. He can jump off an airplane onto asphalt or get on a motorboat; he's never lost anything from the frame. To me he's one superior cameraman as well as an unusual director. Haskell's a man who just takes a hand-held camera and uses it like a paintbrush. On *Medium Cool,* Haskell used his camera to show a portrait of American life, especially when the convention started.

I feel that three pictures — *The Greatest Story Ever Told, Medium Cool,* and *Funny Girl* — are the highlights of my career as an assistant director. I had the opportunity to work with a director of Stevens' quality and artistry on a big screen production. Then there is Wexler, who knew how to bring impact and drama to the screen without the theatrics, and Wyler's understanding of both his artists and crew.

DUTIES OF AN ASSISTANT DIRECTOR

I worked on other shows besides features and television — training films, promotional and documentary-type things. The March of Dimes organization made documentary films at the hospitals to show to their groups, and remember, they had chapters set up all over the country. So they would go out and raise funds with these films, showing them to their volunteers, their coworkers and their fundraising staff, as well as their sponsors and potential donors. This was before they had a telethon.

Arco Oil made a documentary to be shown to their sales people. Industrial film was a field I wish I had gone into because there is millions of dollars in these industrials. They are always being done for corporations like the Ford Motor Company. Every year they have to make a film about their new models. They have to show it to their manufacturers, dealers, stockholders, and people all over the world, so they put as much money into them as they put into a feature picture. Arco Oil gave me a full motion picture and sound crew. That film illustrated franchising opportunities for blacks. We filmed a gasoline filling station that was owned here in Los Angeles, one in Chicago and one in Atlanta, showing these men, their stations, and the type of business they owned. Many companies do these types of films. Industrial film is a big, big world, and a number of blacks are involved in making them. Many black companies use industrial films to advance their products. *Ebony* has put out a film on its company. There are one or two funeral homes that are black-owned in America that put out industrial films on their companies.

I directed a film when a black fraternity had an affair in San Francisco. We shot for three days. In addition to directing, I also worked as a first assistant and unit manager on other shows as well.

Blacks have never had the opportunity to direct many things and we still don't. Now some people like Fred Williamson, have set up their own companies like Masai, and have been able to promote themselves to do documentaries and industrials. I have never seen any of their work, but I do know that they obviously made a living, because they're still in business. The majority of commercials are still made by Madison Avenue kinds of people. I worked on a couple of Chevrolet commercials when NBC had the Chevrolet account. I was first assistant, and unit manager for the Tang commercials. All of them were done in Los Angeles and one of them featured Kareem Abdul Jabbar.

Commercials are a long way from features, they're really in a field of their own. You have a storyboard in a commercial, and that's what they shoot. There's a lot of confusion about commercial storyboards and feature storyboards. Television shows and feature films are laid out the same way, but the time factor and shooting schedules are radically different. In television, you plan two or three pages on the board and then you shoot what's on that board for that day. On a feature film, you can tell what an actor is going to be doing ten weeks down the line, because it's scheduled in that way, the same with TV.

A commercial is usually cast by an agency and nine-tenths of the people in the agency come out on the set and tell you how to shoot it, because they storyboarded it. They lay it out in the same manner that a cartoon is laid out in the Sunday paper. Every shot is told in sketches, and that's what the director shoots. If he's a bigtime director, the agency people don't tell him what to do, but there are some agency people who are also directors. They have the storyboard and they've planned it with their clients, so they know what to shoot. The relationship between the commercial and the feature is just as remote as infantile paralysis is from cancer. I had to learn about commercials by going to school on the set with agency people.

The only way you can shoot a motion picture is with the production board, the breakdown of the show. Every scene is broken down and stripped — how many people are in, say, scene 154 — principal actor one, principal two and whoever else that scene calls for. It's all numbered and broken down onto one strip. The next strip might be totally different because you're shooting out of sequence — you might shoot the middle or the end of the picture before you even get to do the beginning. All of the vehicles, horses, dogs, children, and extras are listed on the strip that you're going to use in that scene.

The assistant director or the unit production manager must transfer that breakdown of the show to paper. Remember this whole thing is published when you go into production. This gives information to the leading man, the prop man, and the hairdresser about what we are going to shoot on, say, July 15th. They need advance notice in order to prepare a different sort of hairstyle or set. That's why you have production meetings.

First, you get the shooting script. Then you assign each scene a number on a strip and you lay it all out on a board. Now you have to plan things with double "L"s — logically and logistically. You've got to be careful because the budget is totally based on that board. You just don't take a script and say, "Oh, I'll just shoot it this way." You arrange it to make the best use of the actors and crew. How can I schedule the two star actors so that there will be a constant shooting of them throughout the entire show? I can see that on the board. I can walk in the office and look up at the board and see that the first star works the first, second, third, fourth, fifth, sixth, seventh days, right across the whole board. The second star works the second, third, fourth days only. Where they overlap is where the money of the show goes. Then way down I have an artist, Joe Simolean, who doesn't work until the twenty-fifth. We don't hire him until the morning of the twenty-fifth of the following month, and that all goes on that board.

From the board, the director sees what he's going to shoot today. When he goes home that night after shooting, he has a call sheet, which carries the information of that production board, including what scenes he's going to shoot tomorrow. The director and the cinematographer have to order the equipment they will be using in advance. So the director takes that home and knows what to study. He or she knows that they have to shoot these twenty scenes and so he studies and he breaks it down as to how to shoot it. All this comes from the assistant director's board layout, which came from the shooting script.

Some directors also use storyboard artists to sketch the scenes, like in a commercial. But in commercials, they don't necessarily have a script because the agency has storyboarded every detail. They shoot the commercial in only one or two days. It's altogether different from motion pictures when it comes to dramatics, they're shooting all this for a thirty-second commercial. Many of these directors don't see the script until three days before shooting. That's where arguments about preparation time come in. I think there should be more. You can tell on many TV shows that prep time wasn't given to them on the show.

A feature film is as different as night and day from TV, because you're shooting for the big screen, you're not shooting for the little box that you see in your house. The assistant director is one of the most important men in motion pictures. This man could be a director tomorrow morning because he constantly asks the director, which way do you want it? Do you want to go with a master or a half master? After the master, where do you want to start at? As an assistant director, you suggest things and try to save time. The first assistant is involved with the stars, he's involved with the scheduling for the next day and even for the next three weeks. The phone might ring and some actor calls up and asks when should he show up for work. Naturally in big studios they call casting. Then casting calls the stage. The director isn't going to stop shooting to answer the phone call. That is taken through casting and the first assistant who is scheduling the show. The second assistant must always be aware of what the first assistant is doing. The second assistant not only works the set, but when the first assistant has gone home, he's still got a couple of hours' worth of work. He's got to do all of the extras' vouchers, he does the production report, the day's work, how many scenes were shot, etc. He doesn't have to worry about how much film moved because the camera report goes up to the majors in the production office. He's got to turn the back of that sheet over and identify what equipment was used. Camera so-and-so, so many cameras, and the first assistant has already ordered this stuff for the next day. You don't have a bunch of cameras just sitting around, they have to be ordered from the camera department the day before they're needed. How many is decided at a production meeting at ten o'clock that morning for the next day's shoot.

On *Funny Girl*, we had two first assistant directors and two seconds. Al Silvani and I had as many as four and five hundred vouchers to do before we went home. We had the big theater scenes and the audiences and the orchestra and dancers with the showgirls. I would stay on the set with my first, because I learned a long time ago, from George Stevens, when you're an assistant director you stay next to that camera. You stay on that camera. You don't move, regardless of how much paperwork you've got to do. Even if the dolly rolls over your foot, you stay next to that camera.

I'll never forget when Stevens was saying something to me, I was so ambitious to get away to fulfill this, he let me go halfway across the stage and he says "Wendell!" I said, "Yes, Mr. Stevens," and I walked back. He said, "You stay here until I finish talking. I never said I was finished. You've taken it for granted." That was some of the discipline that Stevens taught me. Sometimes when you're just starting you can be very impetuous. I wanted to do everything just right, and by being overzealous and trying to do everything right, you did everything wrong. That can happen with anybody.

If you're going on location, you have to notify the chief of transportation about how many vans and buses and extra cars you'll need and when. The unit manager has secured all the permits. In the meantime, he's taken the director out somewhere, sometime during the shooting day for an hour to find out if the director likes the location. The unit manager has previously gone out with his Polaroid and gone out and shot fifty different locations and asked the director what does he think about them. Then there's the price, which has to be run by the producer. Maybe this club costs us five hundred dollars and the other club costs a thousand dollars. Now the producer and director have to knock minds together and decide which place they are going to rent for the day. Nine-tenths of all directors today still have to take orders from their producers. The producer is the person who raised the money, liked the script, and who feels that the script should be interpreted in a specific way. There is always an argument on the issue of creativity, a kind of tug of war between the director and the producer.

The director's been out and looked at one club, and found a place for cameras to move in and out, satisfied himself about all the logistical problems of a location — will we be able to wheel a dolly through it, will it get through the doors?, etc. The electrician has to go out and see if he can light it, maybe these people have beautiful hardwood paneling and they are not going to let you nail those beams and wires up in their ceilings. Shooting motion pictures involves a lot of common sense, and this can't be taught in school.

On *Funny Girl*, we were shooting out at the Crocker estate in Pasadena, using it for the Long Island home of Fanny Brice. The front of this gorgeous mansion was a half acre of lawn which was all clover, fabulous grass it was. Some of the crew jumped off the truck and started hauling their equipment and big rollers across the lawn. Everywhere they walked you saw these great big tracks. It cost the studio about five thousand dollars to replace that lawn.

Some people go into beautiful homes and they just start nailing into the great gorgeous hardwood, but the majority of the top shows know to lay paper over the floors first. The unit manager has gone out and planned all this with the first assistant. When the company goes in that morning the place is prepared. The crew might have been brought out the day before to lay paper on the hardwood floors, the lighting gaffer has been out to see how he can light and where he can light and where the generator is going.

Directors, in this regard, have got to depend on their first assistant director. Cecil B. De Mille kept Chico Day on all his big pictures like *The Ten Commandments* — it became a marriage between them. Frank Capra and William Wyler also carried their assistant directors with them from show to show. They work for the director.

All this experience I've had over the last thirty years has been greater than a college education. I've been with the greatest of directors and each one is a different individual. Only in television have I seen some of these young directors trying to mimic. In features, everybody's observing everyone else's work. But when they decide this is the picture they want to do, they begin to dream and fantasize what they want to see on that big screen. Ultimately, they try to bring that to the set the next day. Some directors walk on the set and say, "I'm shooting this many cuts in this many scenes. On scene 124, I'm shooting nine different cuts and this is how I'm going to cover the shots." Some directors do it from instinct. Then you have the directors who turn around and say, "Hey, which way do you think I should go?" So there's no two alike.

There's no formula for a first assistant director either, because working with a director, the assistant must get to know how that director ticks. The assistant is responsible not only to the director, but to the front office as well. The second assistant acts as a liaison for the business relationships on the set. He handles logistics like which actors are in make-up, when will other actors be out of make-up, which actors are on the set, and which actors must be ready on that stage. The first assistant can not leave that camera. Some never go to the bathroom till the end of the day, and many a first assistant director has developed piles. That's true. You can not leave the set. He can't say in the middle of a take, "Cut! I've got to go to the restroom." Everybody thinks that this business is all horseplay. They read about the glamour — but that's when the picture is over and in the can, six to eight months after the picture has been shot.

One thing I have never had the chance to be involved with is editing. I feel that this has been a misfortune in my career. The directors on features are allowed this opportunity, but a lot of the directors in television, they get a first cut, maybe. When a director like Stevens walks in, he sees thousands of feet of film, and works with the editor to see how it all blends. Editing is an art in itself. I know a couple of directors who keep editors with them on the set, and question them about shots and angles. On the other hand, there are many directors who only know that this is a camera and it shoots film.

Not many assistant directors get the chance to direct, like I did with *Bus*. You don't really move up in position much when you're working behind the camera. Generally, the studio doesn't allow for that. In the offices, yes maybe. You might move up from second AD to first, like Charles Washburn did when I left *The Bill Cosby Show*. Cosby raised him, but it wasn't automatic. It's still a matter of politics, circumstances and personalities that decide, "Well, I'm going to take Joe Shmo and raise him up to first." There are some second assistants that have been seconds for thirty or fifty years. There are some people who have never become a director. It takes somebody who loves you. You don't get promoted to directorship. If I'm a producer and I think that you have talent, then I will hire you as my director by putting up the money for your Guild fees to work on my picture. The Guild doesn't know what your background is or what your academics are like, it has nothing to do with that. Hollywood film-making is not like the outside world, because even some of the young actors today have never been to drama school or had any type of higher education, period.

Jim Brown and other black athletes became actors, and even O.J. Simpson became an actor-producer. Kareem Abdul Jabbar has been in films, so it isn't always the studying of Lee Strasberg and method acting that makes an actor. A lot of people have just said, "Hey, I think you can do the job."

People think that going to all these drama schools is automatically going to put them in pictures, and that isn't true. It's the hustling, the bustling, trying to get yourself an agent, who can really sell you. You've got to have some talent. There are some people who make it, and they used to claim it was the casting couch, but I don't think that it's the only thing going on. Nepotism has a lot to do with it, whether you're black or white.

I've seen very few extras come to be movie stars. Some people come from Broadway and others have "that look." It's a natural talent that exists with people, and maybe I'm wrong, but I don't believe that you have to go to drama schools all your life. You either have it or you don't have it.

Working in features was the only way I wanted to be in this business. I've always felt television to be a rat race, which it still is. But there were two or three incidents in television I loved.

Doing *The Bill Cosby Show* was a great pleasure. It was a new kind of experience working for Cosby, a black man who knew what he wanted. He knew and felt the nuances of life that made his show a success. I do say this, he put the first integrated production crew together. I was the second choice as the first assistant to the show. Luckily for me, Reuben Watt, now deceased, was involved in a feature film at the time. For my second assistant I had a fellow black; Joe Wilcott, the assistant cameraman, was black — he's now a head cameraman. The assistant to props was black, and in wardrobe it was the same thing, chief captain of transportation was black, and all other personnel were white. This was at Warner Bros.

I value Bill very much because he was not preaching separatism, he was not trying to prove anything, he just put qualified people together, regardless of whether they were black or white. This was one of the first integrated crews, which was unusual enough to put us on the front page of the *Calendar* section.

I worked on Bill's show for the first season. He rekindled the careers of many of the black actresses who had been in the black film exploitation period and then given no other work — women like Ketty Lester, Beah Richards, and Rosalind Cash. He used top comedians like Moms Mabley, Mantan Moreland, and fabled character actor Rex Ingram.

He was an integral part of his show, I think that's the reason why he has the success he does now. He not only produces the show, but he gets into it. He has a canny feeling about what works and doesn't work, so his director walks in and respects him. Jay Sandrich has been doing his shows for a long time — they have almost a brotherly relationship on the set.

That's one of the first experiences I had working with a black type of show, but it wasn't all black. We had white kids, Japanese kids, and Mexican kids. This is what motion pictures should be all about, different kinds of people of all races. Cosby was the star and his girlfriend in the series was black. This in itself was a history making event in television.

DIRECTING: *THE BUS IS COMING*

I felt the need to fulfill my dreams of being a black director. On the set of *The Greatest Story Ever Told,* I had been told about this black man who was making a motion picture. They told me he had SAG actors, full union paid cameramen and was shooting out on the streets of Los Angeles. I didn't believe it. But fortunately I met Horace Jackson, who has been a lifetime friend. He had made a picture, *Living Between Two Worlds,* which I had the pleasure of presenting at the Directors Guild to an invitational audience of Charlton Heston and members of the media — it was a packed house. Unfortunately, *Living Between Two Worlds* didn't go far, but this man had the courage and the nerve to try to compete within the industry of motion pictures.

In the early seventies, Horace Jackson sought me out. Things were down in the industry and I was unemployed again, which is almost part of the job description in our business. Horace said he wanted to make a motion picture and he asked me to direct. Well, being a member of the Guild, I knew he did not have the money even to pay me scale. But he sat me down and said, "Man, as black men we're just going to tighten our belts and do a picture." As my producer, Horace cast *The Bus is Coming*. To me, Horace Jackson is one of the few black producers that's been really involved in the making of his films. Here is a man who has gone and raised his own money, made his own film. He personally went to the different production houses and got props, guns, and cars.

In the meantime, there were other men who were thinking about doing the same thing: Melvin Van Peebles, Ivan Dixon, Oscar Williams, Hugh Robertson and a few others. Here was a group of men who had been a part of the civil rights movement, and who felt that they wanted to make films for the black market. They sought out financing from the industry and the banks, but were told, "Hey forget it, blow it out your mind, there is no black market."

That proved to be a lie, and I'll just cite the experience I had in directing *The Bus is Coming*. We started with a small office on Melrose Avenue, but as the script was being developed, Horace and I decided to move to Compton out to Dootsy Williams' Civic Center. We went to the police department and all these people in the Compton area — "Could we shoot here? Could we shoot there?" — and we told them what we were trying to do. Horace is a producer who produces. With his bulldog-like tenacity, he went to SAG and got deferments, went to Eastman Kodak, went to Mirisch Brothers, and went to all the camera companies. We wound up with almost everything being donated to us because we were daring to make a motion picture. Of course, we ran out of money but we did get rescued.

At the very end of *The Bus is Coming* is a biblical inscription, and there's a story behind that. It came about due to Horace being a minister and a beautiful person. He got out of the ministry soon afterwards. We were trying to raise money, so we invited every minister in the city for lunch at the studios we had in Hollywood before we moved to Compton. We had it catered with a full bar. The preachers got drunk, drank up all that cognac, bourbon and scotch and wouldn't give one red penny. So don't tell me about all these people, my people. They drank up and ate and lallygagged, and talked up a storm, but none of them went back to their pulpits and said to their congregation "Let's help these young men." It doesn't work that way any more. They all build these castles, and stay in their Mercedes. They're no different than the white folks, except the white folks make twice as much as they do.

Across the nation, black independent filmmakers had packed houses with *Sweet Sweetback's Baadasssss Song*, and *The Spook Who Sat by the Door*. They said there wasn't a black market, but then the industry which was financially on its ass at that time, decided to make black films. The result was the so-called blaxploitation films, but I resent the fact that our films are lumped together with those pictures. We financed our own films, nobody gave us money, and none of these films were governed by the industry. So they began to make pictures, *Shaft, Foxy Brown, Cleopatra Jones, Superfly*, etc. With their expertise, their money, their in with distributors, we independents were slowly wiped out.

In the late seventies, I had the pleasure of going back to Universal to do a television show with my good friend Stanley Robertson, who was producing *Harris and Company*. Stanley had been a vice president of NBC, and he started around the same time that I did at NBC. When I was on the parking lot, he was in the mail room. Ivan Dixon directed the show every other week, and it was a pleasure to work with him. Ivan was an actor but he was also a pioneer as an independent director, using his own money to do *The Spook Who Sat by the Door* (1973).

Every one of the black-financed and produced films made money, millions of dollars. Yet there was one crucial area we did not know anything about — distribution — and we were beat at the bank by distributors. Financial reports in *Variety* and *The Hollywood Reporter* stated that *The Bus is Coming* made almost thirteen million dollars on 150-dollar investments. We kept waiting for the checks, but there were no checks. You ought to have seen me in the office in the morning. I was running out to get *Variety,* breaking my neck. I saw figures in trades saying the film had made nine million. The distributors placed a full page ad in *Variety,* saying how much the picture had made. The first check I got was for one thousand four hundred dollars. The distributors were running two or three sets of books on us, telling us we hadn't cleared a profit. I'm speaking from a director's point of view, because we blacks haven't fully arrived yet as directors. I even went into litigation over that film, but there's no regrets because it was a learning experience. I don't want to go into some of the personal problems of *The Bus is Coming,* because my producer and I have had problems like all human beings have their problems.

There was a great reaction of people seeing a poster for *The Bus is Coming* on Sunset Boulevard. Traffic stopped; especially at my name! I got news for you. Wendell Gordon [James] Franklin on a billboard and it was an all-white background with this outstanding red logo. I rode up and down Sunset Boulevard for a full day, backwards and forwards just to look at one billboard on one end of Sunset and another billboard on the other end. I didn't believe it, I really didn't. That was done by the distributor.

The promo tour that we launched throughout the country for *The Bus is Coming* was a fantastic experience. Every TV station, every newspaper was interested. Judith Crist did a review in *The New Yorker* that was fantastic. The *Variety* review that I read was very favorable, and *The Reporter* had a good review, and *The Evening Herald* and *The Los Angeles Times*, and *The Chicago Defender* did a very beautiful article.

The San Francisco Film Festival turned into a personal fiasco. During the question and answer period, some blacks challenged me about my use of 'natural' hairpieces on some of the actors. It wasn't a review of the picture, it was on me. The Oakland newspaper gave me headlines about how I tackled the press up there. I told them the only interesting thing that happened during the whole damn festival was me. No, those were blacks confronting blacks. Later in San Francisco, they held a black film festival sponsored by Bay Area filmmakers. The black radicals there really descended on Gordon Parks, putting him down for *Shaft*.

I believe the black press has been instrumental in furthering black careers, if only in the eyes of the black public. Coverage by the black press is a momentary thing; the press only makes something of you when you're riding hot because you have a picture out, or when you're in the news because you're socially involved. Black columnists could be a great tool in acknowledging the working black director or black technician more frequently. Nobody realizes that in the black world, a black stage manager or an associate director is looked upon with pride; whereas in the white world it's just another man that works on film.

When I read the press, I don't read that much about Ivan Dixon or even some of the younger directors like Robert Townsend, Kevin Hooks, Roy Campanella II, or John Singleton. I only read about them once or twice in the black press, with the exception of Spike Lee, who is regularly featured in *Ebony* and *Jet*. The white press goes out and finds personal stories of these people, their associates, and their social life. In-depth stories should be written so that black youth have something they can read about and write a term report on. There needs to be a constant acknowledgment of these people and an awareness of what their projects are and what they're trying to do. Being in filmmaking is difficult, you almost have to be a Superman, just to keep a job.

I have to give credit for the many articles written about me by black columnists clear across the country, even Billy Roe, who wrote for *The Pittsburgh Courier* years ago. Gertrude Gibson has written a lot and I do give her credit as one of the top columnists, especially for the story on Micheaux. Gertrude Gibson Penlen, that's her full name, and for many years she kept me before the public and I value that. Lillian Cumber was our first theatrical agent in Hollywood and her press columns have been wonderful to me as well. Bill Howard has been wonderful to me in his throwaway sheet. Throwaway sheets in our community mean a lot to us, if you ever see *Scoop, The Wave,* and the others. *Scoop* has been very honorable to me.

Stanley Robertson wrote about the dream that I had for a theater and entertainment complex in the old Boulevard Theater down at 27th and Vermont near Washington. They've torn it down now. I passed by there the other day and I shed a tear. It was one of the most fabulous theaters. I went there as a kid, I lived four blocks from there. It was an all-white neighborhood, in the time that I was growing up, and that's where I won my first talent contest. The Inner City Cultural Center was there to begin with, they could have gotten that theater. I don't know what the circumstances were, but the story died.

I've been fortunate in many ways, because the press has been good to me all these years. Not because I was an outstanding director, but because I was a personality and I think that's the main thing that has kept me in the press. I do come up with ideas, I do come up with subject matter, the Micheaux Award, or fashion shows. *The Argonaut* has carried me. The papers in Glendale and Burbank all carried the Oscar Micheaux event — the DGA's 50th Anniversary celebration — on the front page, and that's just about Klan country.

I have a very blunt personality, which a lot of people don't understand. A lady was saying to me that I'm always putting her down. I wasn't putting her down, but just don't be a flunky for me, I don't have to be nice all the time. I am an outgoing person; I am aggressive, they used to call that ambition, until a black man started being ambitious. Then they said it was aggressive and that you should stay in your place. Well, I don't know what place I'm supposed to stay in. See, at the dinner table if you don't put a place card there, then I'm sorry, I will sit anywhere. Many people don't like that attitude, but I see all these other people here doing it. I see that these white brothers are so aggressive they'll take the teeth out of your mouth to give it to the monkey to wear for the picture, and tell you that they were going to borrow it for five minutes. I think you have to do some things with finesse.

THE SMILING MILITANT

In 1967 I became a part of the NAACP, and I was elected president of the Beverly Hills/Hollywood chapter. A lot of controversy surrounded my presidency. I can truthfully say that I have been one of the few men who was able to sit down with the Alliance of Motion Picture and Television Producers (AMPTP) and the unions to find out when they were going to hire. At this time none of the guilds had set up an apprenticeship program; not the make-up artists, the camera guild, editors association, etc.

At the last meeting I attended, I addressed the Executive Secretaries of the camera and sound unions and asked them when they were going to hire blacks. With me at this momentous meeting was Maggie Hathaway, founder and 13th President of the Beverly Hills/Hollywood branch of the NAACP, and Don Parker of the Directors Guild, along with all the executives on the board of the AMPTP. Even to this day, I feel that I had a great part in instigating the opening of the guilds and the unions for blacks within the industry, yet nobody has ever acknowledged me for these things. There is a certain amount of jealousy among people.

I became president of that chapter of the NAACP by being an aggressive member, just as you become president of anything. It's always been a controversial position. I am controversial. Maggie Hathaway was controversial. Way back, as early as the forties and fifties, certain organizations berated the industry on its hiring. It's nothing new. There was a luncheon sponsored for Roy Wilkins and myself at the Beverly Wilshire, and we were the only two blacks attending. All the heads of the studios came to discuss the ramifications of hiring and also of making contributions to the NAACP. This was a very successful meeting, and Roy Wilkins told the industry that the president out here, Wendell Franklin, represented the national chapter.

After *The Los Angeles Times* carried the front page series in the *Calendar* section about the industry and affirmative action, I made the statement that it looked like everything was on the way up in terms of integration and employment. The Board of Directors and my fellow members didn't like my statements. I felt I had done my job, but after that point, I said forget it. I resigned the presidency. They didn't like the idea that I made such positive statements. I guess they wanted me to say that the situation was terrible. Up to this day, I get these mailings that say how the NAACP is monitoring [African-American hiring statistics]. They're still trying to integrate the industry. However, we've got a whole new generation that does not know that all this happened. Just like in our Guild. We have almost 350 minority members and 85 percent are black. Nobody jumps on the bandwagon with the DGA, with the Ethnic Minorities Committee and the apprenticeship program, but the fact is, that the DGA gets quarterly reports.

The Directors Guild has been the leading exponent of fair play in the industry. Now I don't see the NAACP doing anything about the Writers Guild. Once in a while you hear some noise, and that's it. There no way that anybody's going to break Hollywood now. If you asked every black in America not to go to the movies, you'd be a fool, because they're going to the movies. Movies have been one of the greatest escape mechanisms in the world for poor people, since the Depression.

I do criticize the public. We don't write. There's a lot of apathy in the black public of twenty-five million. If five million took the time to write a note on their favorite television show, *The Bill Cosby Show*, or whatever, that would be news. Even if a show features a little five minute, or fifteen minute scene of an actor, like Beah Richards, Rosalind Cash, Cicely Tyson, Ruby Dee, Ossie Davis, or Bill Marshall, that actor would be in demand. What would it do to send five thousand letters to that studio? The white folks do write the studios. Many a show has been saved from cancellation by the public out there.

I've heard it said that back in the early seventies, when I was the head of the NAACP, people in the industry referred to me as "the smiling militant." Well, I never thought of myself as a militant. If you look up "militant" in the dictionary it says a militant will do anything to prove his theory or his philosophy, up to assassination and killing. I've been outspoken, I will always be outspoken till they put me in Forest Lawn or wherever, the potter's field. But I'm trying to be outspoken for the young people who are following behind me. This has been resented by many men of my age level in this industry, who came through the twenties, thirties, and forties — times when you stayed in your place.

A smiling militant, no, but I hope I have a personality. If somebody doesn't speak up, I don't understand that. I guess being a big mouth has denied me a lot of opportunities, but it sure opened up opportunities for other people. They said, "Damn him, we'll take the other person, because they don't say things like that." I know one particular assistant director behind me who the studios would say, "Get him, he's a nice person." But they found out he wasn't a nice person eventually. He found out another second assistant director had changed his whole production report, so he got hot under the collar and grabbed the guy.

I was taught as a child to speak up. There were some circumstances where people would tell me I'm supposed to stay in my place. I don't know what place I'm supposed to stay in, as long as I am a gentleman. I feel that I have a right to speak if something is wrong. I've walked on sets and have said "You don't have any blacks, Hispanics or Asians on the show." Then all of a sudden, they say "Oh yes, well we must have this." There have been many first assistant directors who have been guilty of an all-white complex on some of these pictures. They are the ones to decide the casting for extras. Then when they have a black extra walk on the set and he or she says, "Hey man, ain't none of us here except one or two," the crew pretends to be busy and ignores them.

I'm not fighting for a black world in motion pictures. I'm fighting for fairness, and that's the only thing I know. This is America, and wherever they are, I am. When I walk into supermarkets, banks and practically any venue in America, I see ethnic minorities. The only true picture on the screen can be if you've got them in it. For over seventy-five years, it was as if there were no Chinese, Mexicans, or blacks that even lived in this country. There's twenty-five million people out there that are black. There are millions of Hispanics and Asians. They go to the theater and they deposit their six dollars to go to the movies. There's no director and no producer that can sit back and ignore them, because if it wasn't for the people out there they couldn't be sitting pretty in Brentwood or Beverly Hills. Many people have told me I was wrong for being so loud. I was supposedly defeating myself, I could have gone here and I could have gone there, if I would have kept my big mouth shut.

You could say that this attitude has not worked well for me in Hollywood. I don't care if you're Lew Wasserman, you're just another man as far as I'm concerned. Now I may respect you and your position, but I found myself saying "Mister" to people a lot younger than I am. Now that I've been around for a while, I find out that it's George and Bob and we all go by first names. I had to earn that respect also. I've been accused by members of the industry that I've acted as quite a grand boy, and I am. I'm known as the man with the K.M.B.A. attitude — kiss my black ass! I'm going to have a T-shirt made up that says that I'm a member of the K.M.B.A. society and let somebody ask me what it is! If I ever get an extra few hundred dollars I'm going to make them up. I know quite a few people who could wear that shirt.

DGA ETHNIC MINORITY COMMITTEE

After my resignation from the NAACP, I went on to work in creating the Ethnic Minority Committee of the Guild, with Ivan Dixon as the first chairman and Reuben Watt and, later, William Crain. The primary reason why the Ethnic Minority Committee was formed was to establish the legal grounds to fight for hiring. We didn't get out there and scream "You got to hire us!"; we did it all legally. Reuben Watt and myself appeared before the National Board that was convening at the National Headquarters in Hollywood. At this time Ivan Dixon was serving on the National Board and was the first black to do so; Gordon Parks was on the Directors Council.[1]

Reuben and I presented to the National Board the fact that blacks and minorities were not being hired. We played to a packed house. Reuben was shaking and turning red in the face; people thought that he was going to hit them upside the head with that chair at the conference table. Sheldon Leonard said, "I know when that man is mad; he's mad." But Reuben was the kind who never loses his temper. See, I was the radical; we were always the two blacks in the Guild and he was the nice person.

---

[1] The DGA National Board approved formation of the Ethnic Minority Committee on August 16, 1980.

Some board members claimed that there was no discrimination within the industry. We proved that wrong and we threatened to expose their misguided justification for the lack of employment and the fact was that the Guild had never taken steps to help alleviate this problem. Well, through this confrontation with the National Board, the Ethnic Minority Committee was organized. The women members of the Guild had already organized, and had gained a certain momentum in the media about the lack of hiring of women, especially women who were not minority women. This Women's Steering Committee had already been to the National Board to discuss hiring practices. In a way, we were following their lead.

Reuben Watt and myself gathered together the entire membership list, because at that time the Guild did not separate racial categories. We sent out a survey to all members about their racial backgrounds, and found out that between the east coast and the west coast we had two hundred and seventy-two minority members. Out of this group we formed the Ethnic Minority Committee with the full backing of the Guild and Michael Franklin, Warren Adler and I think our president at that time was Jud Taylor. [Taylor became president in 1981. —Ed.]

After becoming a part of the Guild structure, the Minority Committee went into conferences with the executive staff. Michael Franklin, Executive Director, and the Executive Committee talked with the attorneys about the possibility of entering a fair employment practice suit with the Equal Employment Opportunity Commission (EEOC) based upon affirmative action legislation that had passed the Supreme Court. The Guild was behind us a hundred percent, maintaining lawyers for us and pursuing the legal battle through to the Ninth Circuit Court.

The DGA (through the Women's and Minority committees) had received right-to-sue letters from the EEOC. So the studios were threatened with going into federal court over alleged wholesale discrimination. As a result, the major studios and independents associated with the Alliance of Motion Picture and Television Producers (AMPTP) agreed to sit down in an attempt to try and settle the problem in-house. That delayed our plans to go ahead with the lawsuit.

The strategy of the two committees was to set up conferences with all the major studios, with the minority and women members attending, with the aim of bringing about work. There were problems with the studios over the ground rules. The DGA insisted that more than half the studios had accepted the idea of numerical goals and timetables as a pre-condition to the talks. The producers stated emphatically that none of the studios could have accepted any pre-conditions.

Goals and timetables was a very well-used tool in many affirmative action plans and would establish a flexible minimum hiring level for women and minorities within an established time frame. The AMPTP would not agree to include goals and timetables in the agreement. Through further meetings we decided that we would not come to any conclusions or any agreements without goals and timetables as part of an overall agreement.

Over half of the companies agreed to the concepts. Many of the producers held out and eventually we were forced to bring back the major film studios to the bargaining table.

We were backed up into a corner and we were going to sue. Their argument was that they didn't need goals and timetables. Yet before 1980, there were no timetables and goals and they still wouldn't hire anybody.

We were forcing them, telling them there's affirmative action outside in the corporate world, even though that was a long time coming. By the 1980s affirmative action had been well established in civil service and some of the commercial firms like Arco Oil, who were making money from the black consumer. Some they made managers and some they provided with service station franchises. But the motion picture industry remains a very closed world — it's run on a corporate basis, but it's run by families, by personal friends and that sort of thing.

Even in the early years, the Directors Guild reflected the prejudices and mores of society at large. How can you look at it any other way? I was the first black man to join the DGA in 1960. I was forty-four years old. There wasn't another black member in the Guild for a long time. I've held the longest membership in the Guild of any black man; we all lived in a discriminating society, period. There were other black directors, including Oscar Micheaux, who did things on their own. Blacks are not a part of mainstream Hollywood. I'm trying to tell young people today that, because there's a myth about Hollywood — but it's a white dream, a white myth, it's not a black dream at all, because we've never been a part of it, except to act as clowns.

The court turned us down not on affirmative action, but on the technicality that we had to sue as individual people. My idea was to sue in New York or Washington, where we had offices. But the Guild wanted to keep it here in the state of California, because this was our national headquarters. Afterwards, I think that Michael Franklin felt that there was some merit in my approach. But our lawyers at the time insisted they knew. We had the clout of one of the strongest organizations in the country, but then we were not allowed to sue as a collective body. This technicality ruling is still in effect. It takes big money to go to the Supreme Court as an individual, but somehow William Crain and two others managed to file civil lawsuits. That was our only recourse, to sue individually. It takes a whole lot of money to sue Warner Bros. You've got to come up with a battery of lawyers. The crux here was that the Guild backed the Ethnic Minorities Committee, we went to court, and it was defeated on a technicality.

Two or three committees were set up that went out and talked with the various producers at the studios. Now I wasn't on any of those, but it was representatives from our Ethnic Minority Committee, along with Warren Adler as legal counsel. It was decided that each studio would provide reports to the Guild every three months. The end result? Some did and some didn't.

As chairman of the Ethnic Minority Committee that instigated all this, Ivan Dixon suffered a backlash. He just couldn't get any work. When I was head of the NAACP, the same thing happened to me — no work. They're scared to death of you running around being an activist. Most of the top blacks who have been activists, how many of them have gotten good jobs? Stokely Carmichael, and all of these people, none of them have jobs.

Many minorities, not only blacks, for some reason are low key and it's their fault. Any time I've ever tried to be part of something in this Guild, I've had no problems. William Crain, Ivan Dixon nor any others have had any problems in seeking out people. At the luncheon, I told Robert Wise that I would like to be on the Foundation Board. That's made up of some of the most prominent names in the field, and they oversee the building and pension fund. Robert Wise said to me, "Well, why not?" I think that one gets too sensitive at times and I know that from experience. We just don't take the initiative to step out there and say, "Hey, I'm here." I think this is very important.

DGA 50TH ANNIVERSARY

In 1986 the Directors Guild celebrated its fiftieth anniversary. I felt very elated and very honored to serve on the anniversary committee along with Jackie Cooper, Howard W. Koch, Lamont Johnson, Arthur Hiller, George Sidney, Joseph C. Youngerman, chairman Robert Wise, and other prominent DGA members. We were sitting around at a noon meeting, and we were debating about what events we would have during the year of celebration. We had mentioned that they were going to honor two great directors — Federico Fellini of Italy and Akira Kurosawa of Japan.

I sat very quietly, gave the "aye" vote along with the rest of the members of the committee, and I went home and I began to ponder what could I suggest that could be celebrated on this historic occasion. I had read about a man, I had seen his pictures as a kid, and this man to me, being a part of the film industry, this man was almost my mentor. He started way back in nineteen hundred and fifteen, he went all the way from silent pictures to sound; a man who produced and financed, and carried and distributed his own films, a man who actually created a national name during the nineteen hundreds, the twenties, the thirties and forties.

I wondered if the prestigious DGA was aware of this man. I had my doubts one way or the other, and I sought as much research material as I could. The following meeting I managed to get the floor, because everybody was busy, but I felt self-conscious. I thought I was being ignored and probably I wasn't, but I finally gained the floor and said, "You know, ladies and gentlemen, I think that there's a man that we should honor. I think that in the industry his films were a counterpart to D.W. Griffith's *Birth of a Nation*, he was a peer to King Vidor, whatever they made in films he turned it around, using black people as a sort of a reflection of what he felt about Hollywood because there were no blacks in films. Whites were blacked up, so he decided to make motion pictures for the black populace of the nation. At that time there was complete segregation, from the teens and even into the forties." I said to the anniversary committee, "The man's name is Oscar Micheaux."

Robert Wise, one of our outstanding Academy Award winners and one of our great directors said, "You need not go any further, we know the man. We will present it to the National Board." Then I thought, "The National Board is made up of mostly younger directors, will they go along with it?"

David Shepard, at the time the DGA's Special Projects Officer, called me and said, "Wendell, the National Board has voted for it, now what are you going to do? Money is no object. It's up to you what you develop to make this one of the events of the fiftieth anniversary." To me, this was fantastic! I couldn't sleep, I had reached back from the year I was born to this man, Oscar Micheaux and at last he was going to be honored by his peers, by the world's directors of the motion picture industry. I could not fathom the magnitude of what I was into. The Guild gave me all the operational staff that I needed and all the facilities.

So we began to search for a film. Eastman Kodak with the cooperation of the Museum of Modern Art and the Directors Guild rehabilitated a film that was Paul Robeson's debut as an actor, *Body and Soul*. We decided to make it an invitational affair with all the glamour that would be deserving to this man, a black American who would be honored by the entire industry.

Invitations were sent out to three hundred of the outstanding blacks within the Hollywood industry and black intelligentsia, but there were only one or two members of the black press present. Now the black press has never said too much about this man. All the networks and television people were there en masse. People were lined up in front of the Directors Guild Theatre for the great tribute. It was very classy, very glitzy, a very elegant audience. At the end of the picture, *Body and Soul*, the curtain came down with Gaylord Carter at that organ, ending with this great big crescendo with the lights coming up slowly. The audience, an outstanding group of artists, teachers, and civic leaders, just sat there for one solid minute completely paralyzed; then all of a sudden the applause rained, giving a standing ovation to a silent screen. I cried, I mean my dream had been fulfilled. I feel this way, I may not ever have all the recognition in the world, but as long as one is filled and satisfied with himself, that's success.

But I wasn't satisfied. With all the cameras, the TV networks and that sort of thing, it was my dream that this man should be enshrined on the famous Hollywood Walk of Fame. I presented this to various members of the executive areas of the Guild. One or two said no, but I didn't give up. I want to thank God for people like David Shepard, Howard Koch, Robert Wise, Michael Franklin,

George Sidney, and Gilbert Cates. I think they had a great esteem in themselves, because there had been more publicity given to the Guild nationally and internationally from the award to Oscar Micheaux than Fellini or Kurosawa. The money came forth, and what a day on Hollywood Boulevard! It seemed Mother Nature cried for days, the rains came down and down. Yet almost five hundred people were in the streets to see this man enshrined. Buddy Collette, one of our world famous musicians put together a jazz group and how they played!

Standing in that rain coming down in torrents, were my fellow Guild brothers, Robert Wise, George Sidney, Gilbert Cates, Michael Franklin, our National Executive Secretary, and the world. The actors were out. Raymond St. Jacques, Moses Gunn — it was a celebrity affair even though it rained and it rained. When we finally unveiled the star, we all were soaking wet. But to me this was a great tribute to a man who did not have a headstone on his grave. Yet, the world can now see that name along with other great directors on the Hollywood Walk of Fame. I feel that this accomplishment was one of the greatest steps in my life.

Maybe I never had the opportunity to make many films, or even think about an Academy Award, but this was my Academy Award night. At last, historians, and children all over America — not only black children — can know that regardless of the racism, that the industry recognized a black man in the world of motion pictures. Now as I walk Hollywood Boulevard at times, my dream is fulfilled and if I do nothing more in life, I've accomplished the deed of recognition for this man who is the father of all black directors.

I had said in the beginning that we would present the award to the Black Filmmakers Hall of Fame in Oakland. This was another great day. The Guild sponsored my trip first class to Oakland, along with my co-chairman William Crain. Gina Gates, a black associate director in television came along; she had helped coordinate the whole affair as well. The press was there, we were received as if we were kings and queens. There were thousands of people in the street. Backstage were many top stars, because this was also Sammy Davis, Jr.'s big day. I'll never forget how I heard my name called as the first black man behind the camera. I walked through this beautiful stage set with all the TV cameras turned on me, and it felt like this was my Academy Award. I presented a replica of the Hollywood Walk of Fame star and the beautiful glass sculpture piece from the Directors Guild, and then received accolades and a plaque from the Hall of Fame in return. Inside of me, I wanted to cry outwardly.

Back at the hotel, Sammy came and put his arms around me and said "Hey, God bless you, my brother." Having met and known Sammy over the years, this was our first acknowledgment to each other that there was a certain amount of beauty and warmth in our existence. Sammy is also a member of the Directors Guild. I felt kindred toward him.

At home, overlooking the balcony to the ocean, I said to myself, in a very strange way, thank you to all the beautiful people at the Directors Guild who sponsored my whole idea for a whole year and a half with not an argument for money, but with the singular attitude of just getting the job done.

The following week, I watched the press and the national newspapers across the country, but in the black press the event was just a small item. Yet the national news carried Micheaux on the front page; *The Los Angeles Times* carried it front page in the *Calendar* section. Even for the Micheaux star installation on the Hollywood Walk of Fame, I only saw a short item in a small weekly black publication. Yet I received newspaper clippings from Sweden, Germany, Africa, and the Caribbean. It was a history-making thing across the world. It was news. It's news when a black man is accepted by his peers. Remember, this man came along with the pioneers of motion pictures from Edison on up. He was a man that died and people forgot about him. Many of his films have been found in garages and tin cans. He was in a world that said, "This ain't the place for you, brother."

Whether consciously or not, the Directors Guild of America has given us a role model for young blacks, some unborn, who want to be a part of this world of filmmaking. I see all these young people today, aspiring and wanting to be in a world that has not really accepted them, on the fringes. Micheaux left them a legend, he left roots. When blacks use this term, they mean it in a very deep way. If he were alive today I think he would say this, "I left roots to black boys and black girls, and as a black man did it the only way I could. Now you have many things that I didn't have, so here it is. Many of you are going to achieve many, many things and someday one of you new directors out there will receive an Academy Award for best picture of the year. But never forget me, Oscar."

LOOKING FORWARD

There can be a black renaissance in film, but we've got to go out there and get the money. The white man is not going to give us any money. In his book, *This Life*, Sidney Poitier says that we must get into positions where we can somehow finance films, maybe through black people of wealth. This point is somewhat dubious, because most investors want a fast turnover for their money. The problem is that blacks are not in the mainstream of the motion picture industry. I'm one of the few black directors who was not an actor first. Many have come by opportunities because they acted on a show and became "in" with their producer. Then they were allowed to direct on a show, and have eventually received directing assignments.

Today, it's a wasteland as far as blacks directing feature films. Despite this, there are a number of young blacks who are directing an episode here and there in television. When a studio asks about a director, they ask if you are experienced. Then they can say "Well, you're not experienced so you're undesirable." How can anybody with two TV shows have a lot of experience? Yet I've seen some white fellows go out of here who hardly knew what a camera was, and they become feature directors. The imbalance is there. There is no excuse for it, because the profile of the consumer who goes to pictures and rents videos includes millions of black people. I'm an American first, and my green money spends, I don't care what color puts its hands on it.

I'll live to see the day when a black in film is not black, he's an American. He's a filmmaker, he just happens to be black. He or she can make films regardless of their content or marketing for the public. I don't think we can specialize in one market; if I cook food for a restaurant I want all the people to come in and buy my food, be they black, white, yellow or whatever.

There are many young people out there now who are going to pave a great road within filmmaking. Their ideas are not so narrowed down to think that it's just a black world. So many of us think all-black. Now this is not true, because we do not live in an all-black world. I'm going to see the day that a black director will be allowed to do a *Greatest Story Ever Told* or a *Grapes of Wrath* or a *Maltese Falcon,* not because of his color, but because he's a good creative, technical man. A black man who can direct an all-white cast on whatever he's being hired for. He's being hired as an artist. Why is it that a black man has to do a black thing? I don't understand that. Never will.

When the first black man wins the Academy Award for best director, I pray that I'm here. If I'm not here, I'm coming out of heaven. I'm going to walk into that premiere from my limousine with my white robes on. I'm going to see that day! If I don't see it, I'll hear it! My white carpet is going to roll down from heaven to the Shrine Auditorium. I remember the day I stood in applause for Sidney Poitier when he won the Academy Award for a dramatic performance, so don't tell me it's impossible! I saw Lou Gossett win the Academy Award for a dramatic performance! Georg Stanford Brown won the Emmy for directing, and John Livingston was nominated for an Oscar. They didn't jump up and down and scratch the dingleberries out of their nose. These were performances, these were not any playthings! The thing is this, we'll always sing, we'll always dance, we'll always be communicative. Black people have an intuition and intuitiveness to act, to sing, we got rhythm. I'm being sarcastic now. But we got a beat, we can interpret many things.

I believe that my people have something that the other man is paid to have, know what it is? Soul, baby. I don't think many people know what soul is. Soul has come through hard knocks, and being kicked around; soul has come from believing in a purpose that I can, I will, I must, I shall. Soul is something they can't take away from you, because it's God-given.

I'm not impressed with all the technologies, all the high tech. You first have to have a mind, you have to have an eagerness, you have to have emotion, involvement. I don't care what they create! A machine can't make a director. If you don't have intuition or a heart with feeling and emotion, or a vision, dreaming how that should become a being and living thing on that silver screen, you're not a director and you can't blow it out of your machine. First place, you got to have a heart and a little bit of soul.

If I had the opportunity to do whatever I wanted now, I'd produce my own feature. I was working with a couple of writer friends and we had it titled *Phylum*, meaning the group, the family. If I had millions of dollars in my pocket, I'd do my own film. I would have to. That's not just an ego trip, I just feel like everybody else — I've got to get my own script. Like every man in this business, a director, producer or whatever feels like he has a script, everybody in a penitentiary has a script. Everybody thinks that their life story is a great thing for the screen. I'm not saying that they're wrong. Of course in everyone's life there would be some interest, there would be some shading. Now to make that entertaining, which is the chief essence of film, it takes writers, and creative distance.

I would like to sit as executive producer on the film and bring in a good producer, and a good director that I would want to sit on camera with.

This script has quality, but I've had problems finding a literary agent, and that's the only way you're going to sell it. I can't just send this out to a thousand people. Even though I have the script, I still don't have the finances. It takes money for rewrites, or seed money, it takes money to go right down here to a copy shop just to make instant copies.

I'd hire a director, because I'd rather be involved with the money. I'm not one to sit up and be happy if people are spending my money. This picture would require a crew of about seventy-five or eighty people not counting the accounting and the upper management people. I'd want to know the day-to-day costs and I'd want to know how much we have spent and how much we will have to spend tomorrow.

I'd like to have Haskell Wexler be my cameraman. I'm not talking about race, I'm talking about talent. I would have an integrated crew, because I feel there would be some people who are just good in their field and it wouldn't matter what race they were. If I was producing they would all have to follow what I wanted to be done.

Each one of these people would be so beautifully involved not just in making a motion picture, but in making it with love. If you watch a picture, you can tell if it's made with love. When you see the actors, there's such blending of relationships, you can almost see it on the screen, and how they look in each other's eyes. Their thoughts are, "Hey, I'm enjoying this film, I'm a part of it." I would be involved in the direction with my director and tell him how I feel, not what to do. I want to show him about twenty pictures that follow my conception of how this picture feels and looks. For example, I really enjoyed what they do with the camera moves in *The Witches of Eastwick*. That's the kind of photography I like.

When people talk about black film directors, they bring up the black films of the seventies. But they were mostly films made with black actors by white directors at the major studios. This is where the expression black exploitation came from. All of Hollywood decided to make black films, once they found out that the black market was a heavy paying market at the box office. Here is where we really discovered we were all pimps, dopeheads, hookers, and gamblers. I turned down two directing jobs because I was not going to do pornography or a "mammy" picture.

That's the kind of movie that was offered to me to direct after I made *The Bus is Coming*, one of the black independent films of the seventies. When we did a picture like *The Bus is Coming*, we were trying to show the injustice of society and things like that. *The Spook Who Sat by the Door* was a political statement. *Five on the Black Hand Side* was a social statement. As a black director and producer, if I have the money and it's my money, I must make a statement about my environment. Every director does, whether they want to admit it or not.

I consider these blacks the "New Pioneers" in film: Melvin Van Peebles, Ossie Davis, Mark Warren, Hugh Robertson, Horace Jackson, and Oscar Williams in the directorial field. These were the first black men to produce and finance their films. Berry Gordy was a pioneer as a producer who finally became a director. Gordon Parks is a role model to me, he's made me want to be what I'm trying to be. He excelled as one of the world's greatest photographers for *Life* magazine, then he came out and did the *Shaft* pictures which were financial boons to a studio that was on its way down. Yet, when they asked him back for the third picture and he asked for points on the picture, they refused him.

There isn't an area in the motion picture business where blacks have not qualified themselves as outstanding technicians. Joe Wilcott and Chuck Johnson are pioneers, our first two cameramen within the industry. I think we have over twenty-seven or twenty-eight young men in camera now, and many people in make-up.

This is a long cry from 1960, when I came into film. I was at the right place at the right time, but I didn't know anything. I had to learn everything the hard way. But now the Directors Guild has an apprenticeship program, the Assistant Director Training Program (ADTP). UCLA, USC and colleges across the country have cinema courses. Black youth today has the advantage of studying cinema in an academic setting, which wasn't happening in the fifties and hardly in the sixties. Today we have almost two hundred and seventy-five minority members in the Guild working behind the camera from director and assistant director to associate director to stage manager, and as production assistants.

This was unheard of until the riots in the sixties. I remember when Universal went down to Watts and picked up a load of black kids and brought them to different areas in various departments from props, transportation, wardrobe and many areas. Universal was the only studio to employ blacks in everything except camera, sound and make-up. At one time during the sixties some of our white brethren called Universal a plantation.

While the Guild has opened up the ADTP, the average black student who graduates out of college is not going to go into the apprenticeship program for the low amount it offers you for two years. Not when he's got a degree in liberal arts or in law or whatever, he can teach or get a job where he can make some money. When I see any blacks going into the apprenticeship program, they're making a big sacrifice, because it's like four more years of college.

I remember how we advertised for the Guild's ADTP in papers all over the country. Reuben Watt and I used to welcome the one or two blacks that were nominated to the apprenticeship program with an evening of food and drinks.

We would see an all "A" student out of the university with an extensive background. He would say, "No way, I don't need this program, because I can go off and make thirty thousand a year right now."

The apprenticeship program is a great sacrifice for many students who think they are going to come out of college and start directing features. But that's not going to happen to someone coming off of the college level where everything has been simplified for you. Nobody's going to gamble that kind of money on you. A lot of directors take their sons out on the weekends on the sets and give them a little firsthand look at things, so in a sense it's a hand-me-down thing, I believe.

Now I realize that autumn is setting upon my horizon, but there are a lot of young people out there, men and women who have the dreams and vision to make motion pictures. They have to learn through the experience of the people from the past, pioneers like Oscar Micheaux, who have tried to open the door and make inroads into the film industry. I hope that in some way I have been a little help and encouragement, being one of the first door-openers to a disenfranchised people within this industry that kept a closed door.

SELECTED TELEVISION AND FILM CREDITS

DIRECTOR

Bus is Coming, The

ASSISTANT DIRECTOR

Art of Love
Enter Laughing
Favor, The [A Very Special Favor]
Fluffy
Funny Feeling
Funny Girl
Gaily, Gaily
Gambit
Greatest Story Ever Told, The
How to Save Your Marriage (And Ruin Your Life)
I'd Rather Be Rich
Incident at Phantom Hill
Kitten with a Whip
Madame X
McHale's Navy
Medium Cool
Model Shop
Munster Go Home
Night Walker, The

Omen II, The
Strange Bedfellows
Three on a Couch
War Lord, The
Who's Minding the Mint?

Television:
Bill Cosby Show, The
Eddie Fisher Show, The (live)
Ellery Queen (live)
Farrady and Son
George Gobel Show (live)
Green Hornet, The
Harris and Company
It Could be You (live)
Martin Luther King Documentary
Matinee Theater (live)
McMillan and Wife
Men Against Evil
Monroes, The
Name of the Game, The
Peyton Place
Racket Squad, The
Tammy Grimes Show
This is Your Life

Stage Manager:
Jerry Lewis Show, The
Nat King Cole Show, The
Queen for a Day
This is Your Life

INDEX

C

E

N

O

P

Q

R

S